OFFICER OR DIRECTOR OF THE FOLLOWING CORPORATIONS, OR MEMBER OF FOLLOWING FIRMS:

Name of Corporations or Firms	Office or Position Occupied by You
Greene & Greene Architects	

BUSINESS OR PROFESSIONAL RECORD

Please furnish here sufficient data to enable the editor to do complete justice to your business or professional record. The facts should be put down in chronological order, beginning with your first occupation. All important business changes and removals, and all firms, business associations and enterprises with which you have been connected should be noted, giving exact dates whenever possible.

Began in Pasadena Jan '93 - Moved principal Office
Los Angeles 1901. Present address 722
Grant Bldg. In Pasadena and Los Angeles
we have built several small business blocks
and several hundreds of dwelling houses.
Our attempts mostly in line of Domestic Architecture
may be arranged in three grand divisions. 1st
To understand as many phases of Human Life as possible
2nd To provide for its individual requirements in the most
practical & useful way. 3rd To make these necessary
and useful things pleasurable. As it may be
conjectured, our ambition over reaches our powers
and hitherto our greatest successes have been mostly
failures. However it has been our good fortune in
the last three years (OVER) to find clients whose ready
sympathy has given us much needed encouragement

Author of the fo............................ address of present
publishers. Please give .... ged in order of date
of publication. If any book is out of p......., ...ely published, please
so state. A printed list of books would assist the editor in securing
accuracy. Enter books only here.

LIST OF BOOKS:

Full Title of Books	Year First Published	Name and Address of Present Publisher

MISCELLANEOUS NOTES

Has Your Biography been published? _____ no _____

Where and when? _____

Any inventions? _____ Photographs of my work in the Fine Arts bld.
of the St Louis World's Fair

Important works in music or art? We also exhibit architectural ....

Names of Children and Dates of Birth Nathaniel
Patrickson Greene Feb 13
1902 Bettie Store Greene
Oct 21st 1903 Alice Sumner
Greene March 6th 1905

To Richard N. Campen
    Greene and Greene for Ohio
    with best wishes from the
    author Janann Strand

        December 1975

A GREENE & GREENE GUIDE

A GREENE & GREENE GUIDE

by Janann Strand

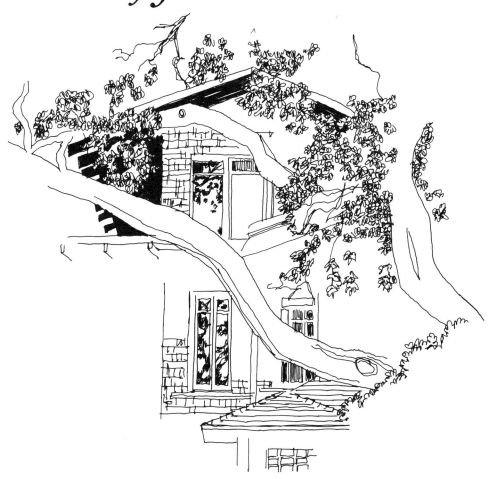

Sketches by Gregory Cloud

Standard Book Number 0-9600780-1-0
Library of Congress Card Number 74-15804
Printed in the United States of America by
Grant Dahlstrom/The Castle Press
Copyright © 1974 by Janann Strand, Pasadena, California

The material in this book is available to the public in a variety of ways. The views that appear as sketches are easily seen from public sidewalks, and the author cautions the reader against misuse of anything in these pages that might jeopardize the continued enjoyment of our architectural heritage. Readers are warned against trespassing upon any of these premises or disturbing or annoying the occupants in any way; although the houses are significant, the people living in them are not prepared to admit visitors or conduct tours.

This book will be mailed postpaid upon request to the author, P. O. Box 2725-D, Pasadena, California, 91105, accompanied by check or money order.

Corrections and suggestions are most welcome.

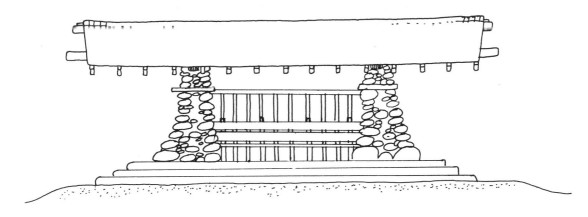

"A Shelter for view lovers to be built on Monk Hill, Pasadena, California, Greene and Greene, Archts, Pasadena, Dec. 3rd '07"

GREENE AND GREENE ARCHITECTS

*"An architect, who is asked to build a house
to go upon the sea, must not build a Parthe-
non, or a square house, but a ship."*[1]

THE ARCHITECTURAL FIRM of Greene and Greene (1893-1922) created an architectural form that has become indigenous to the southern half of California; theirs is not an anonymous art. Charles Sumner Greene and Henry Mather Greene were an integral part of their creative time and place, and although part of a continuum and indebted to other influences, "Greene and Greene" evokes a unique image. This image has, in turn, exerted considerable influence upon the architects of sub-sequent years, not solely in southern California, and encouraged a "Greene and Greene" mythology. The contents of this guide set forth what they did, what they said, and how they were regarded by some of their contemporaries. This is an invitation to a firsthand interpretation.

[1] Ralph Waldo Emerson, Beloit, January 9, 1856, JOURNALS OF RALPH WALDO EMERSON: 1820-1876, Vol. 9, 1856-1863, Edited by Edward Waldo Emerson and Waldo Emerson Forbes, p. 8. Houghton-Mifflin Co., Boston and New York, 1913.

I   Acknowledgments

IT IS A DELIGHT to credit Gregory Cloud, B.A. in Architecture, School of Architecture and Fine Arts, University of Southern California, for the skill and enthusiasm with which he did the sketches and plans that illustrate this book.

The name Greene and Greene appears in print extensively, starting in 1896. Randell Makinson's study, in FIVE CALIFORNIA ARCHITECTS, lifts the Greenes from an aesthetic eddy and sets them in an appropriate relation to California architectural history. The appreciation of their contribution up to this point was mainly local, professional, or ephemeral. Curator of The Gamble House, Mr. Makinson is the author of the lead essay in the issue of *The Prairie School Review* devoted to The Gamble House. Until the publication of a comprehensive study of the Greenes, these two publications and his excellent Docent Training Lectures deserve first acknowledgment. He is to be thanked for his focus upon Greene and Greene for eighteen years, beginning with a Rehmann Fellowship for research in 1956.

Esther McCoy, editor and critic, has synthesized the Greenes' philosophy, skill, and technique into what she describes as their design vocabulary; her book, FIVE CALIFORNIA ARCHITECTS, grew out of an earlier exhibit and catalog of the work of seven architects practicing on the West Coast (Neutra and Frank Lloyd Wright were included, as well as Maybeck, Gill, Schindler, and the Greenes). For this and other publications, she is credited by Gebhard and Winter in their GUIDE TO ARCHITECTURE IN SOUTHERN CALIFORNIA with a 'one-woman Crusade' on behalf of West Coast architects; Reyner Banham repeats their praise, as does this author.

Some of the liveliest prose in behalf of the Greenes is that of writer Jean Murray Bangs, wife of the architect Harwell Hamilton Harris, who gathered a great deal of source material in preparation for a book (not published) in the 1940s and 1950s. She also helped to arrange an exhibit of their work at the Biltmore Hotel in Los Angeles in 1948, when the Greenes were awarded a Special Certificate of Merit by the Southern California Chapter of the American Institute of Architects. The source material, which Mrs. Harris sent to the Avery Architectural Library, Columbia University, in 1960 and 1961, has been available to all who are seriously interested in plans and construction details. This is to express gratitude for the use of these resources.

Kenneth Cardwell, University of California at Berkeley, deserves a special thanks for his graciousness and generosity, which were so encouraging long before any thought of a book. Three architectural librarians have been helpful in significant ways: Arthur B. Waugh, University of California at Berkeley; Adolph Plazcek, Columbia University; and Alson Clark, University of Southern California, whose unfailing helpfulness and good humor have benefited The Gamble House in many ways. In addition, David Gebhard, University of California at Santa Barbara, Robert Winter, Occidental College, and William

Current, with his fine photographer's eye, have given timely assistance.

Without the superior facilities of the Pasadena Public Library, this guide would have been almost impossible. Thanks go to Mrs. Elizabeth Keith, Reference, Mrs. Lan Wu, Miss Joyce Penny; and Josephine Pletscher, Fine Arts Coordinator, whose green notebooks have fattened with material in her pioneering efforts to record architectural history in Pasadena. The South Pasadena Library deserves mention for its willingness to obtain source references not available locally. Friends from Japan to Germany and points between have shared an interest in the effort to gather this information.

Douglas Byles, AIA, has been planning architectural tours in and for Pasadena for over twenty years, this is a welcome opportunity to thank him for the inspiration he has provided for Greene Walks.

Roy H. Copperud, author and Professor of Journalism at the University of Southern California, cheerfully accepted the challenge of copy editing, and Enid Bell neatly turned her several skills from science to architecture. Thanks, and welcome to two new Greene Walks recruits!

And praise to James Gamble, who continues the generous client tradition set by his grandparents in 1908.

DEDICATION

To the Docents of The Gamble House

The Initial Docents, who pioneered a new concept.

The Charter Docents, who did everything for the first time.

The Present Docents, who expand and refine

And the Future Docents, who will . . .

Table of Contents

Charles Sumner Greene

Henry Mather Greene

Introduction

ARCHITECTURE is a three-dimensional art. When it is confined to two dimensions (as in a book), the vital third is missing. One must move into framed space to discover the significant dimension. The architecture of half a century ago — even though described and documented as in this guide, and viewed and visited — also lacks a significant dimension. But that dimension is irrecoverable.

It is the matrix of streets and structures in which the Greenes lived their lives, the total fabric to which they related and reacted, and in response to which they designed. There is no way to wholly reconstitute that matrix, for one would have to start two centuries back and on older shores — England, then Philadelphia, Wyandotte (Virginia), St. Louis, Boston, Chicago, San Francisco, and, ultimately, early Pasadena.

Here we cannot replace Pasadena's Brookside Park with woodlots, dairies, and a bouldered stream shaded by sycamores; nor scrape down the century of trees to gentle grassy hills; nor build again the board-and-batten barns, the dispersed structures, citrus-encircled — Pasadena at the turn of the century. "... We cannot NOT know history,"[1] and something does not come from nothing; it comes from something. In this year of 1974 we shall try to evoke that matrix into

(All footnotes appear at the close of the Introduction.)

which the Greenes were set. The historical perspective acts as a prism.

The concept of The Detached House is very new, architecturally speaking. Older however than the railroad station (1830s), the skyscraper (1880s), or the shopping center (1940s), it developed with the emerging middle class in late Medieval England. "In the long story of man's dwellings from prehistory to the present, the Anglo-American development that took place in the hundred years between the 1790s and the 1890s is of considerable significance, particularly as it provides the immediate background of the twentieth-century house ..." Henry-Russell Hitchcock, in ARCHITECTURE: 19th AND 20th CENTURIES, explains how the yeoman's home became larger, the villa became smaller and a new stratum emerged, the suburban dwelling. The early eastern seaboard in America provided ample opportunity for English colonists building the houses they knew best. The emerging colonial stature is clearly visible in a heritage of homes from the Parson Capen house (1683, Topsfield, Massachusetts) through Mount Vernon (1787) to the Andrews House of 1872 [Andrews sketch].

Nearly paralleling this development was the Picturesque point of view, encouraging the eclectic as well as the original, and offering a spectrum of choices limited only by what could actually stand as built, the ultimate test of any structure. What could not be put on the house was put into it, and in the rush to embrace Nature by a nation too young and vigorous to have a seasoned architectural mode of its own, the countries of the world were borrowed from — the pitched roof and broad eaves of the Swiss Chalet, towers from Italian villas, bay windows from the Tudor parsonage, verandas from Bengal, and articulated structure from the Orient. (Interesting variations of the tower form may be found in many Greene and Greene houses, often barely discernible.)

Coming into this milieu from a youth spent in the Virginia countryside, Charles and Henry Greene studied to become architects. Their experience of nature had been rural; their response was therefore to those elements embedded in 19th-century architectural theory that were organic and natural. The lessons of architectural history and form absorbed at the Massachusetts Institute of Technology refined this response until it flowered later in California into a very personal aesthetic. The inchoate development of American architecture from about 1840 fed upon a growing tradition of organic reality which aligned itself with the burgeoning qualities of individualism and articulation. The result was a building form compatible with the earth, not alien upon it; an invitation to wind and sun and shadow, the forms and colors of the earth; and made of wood, which was plentiful. Vincent Scully calls some of these wooden houses of the fifties and sixties the "stick style," those of the seventies and eighties the "shingle style." In a leap for architectural freedom, "the house stretches out to cover the ground, bursting through partitions inside, extending porches outside . . ."

The American middle-class house could not have developed before the invention of the balloon frame technique of the 1830s. (The skyscraper could not have been built before steel and the elevator of the 1880s: in another leap for architectural freedom the office building reached for the sky — straight new American steel, but

hung with classical trappings.) Paralleling this was the wooing of that constant muse, the Beaux Arts discipline and formalism emanating from academies for proper architects and their new professional organization, the American Institute of Architects. Looking backward from 1913, Ralph Adams Cram describes the academic way of working from the outside in, planning an obdurate shell into which accommodations were stuffed. "So long as this custom continued we had many houses, but little real architecture . . ."[2] Planning from the inside out is the American contribution to The Detached House.

Studying at Calvin Woodward's Manual Training High School in St. Louis, the Greenes were beneficiaries of one of the most creative ideas in education around the turn of the century. Elevating handwork to the status of art, Woodward promoted principles, rather than products of wood, metal, or the machine; the progressive coordina-

Andrews House, H. H. Richardson, Newport, Rhode Island, 1872.

tion of the hand with the mind. As William Jordy says in AMERICAN BUILDINGS AND THEIR ARCHI-TECTS, "whereas the starting point for Greene and Greene was the craft, for Wright it was the geometry. Manual training versus Froebel blocks: it was a difference of kindergartens, so to speak."[3]

Rarely has anyone writing about the Greenes failed to explain their sensitivity to the inherent qualities of materials, the enrichment of the essential construction, and the absence of features that served only "propriety" or "convenience." Yet these principles were advanced in 1841 by A.W.N. Pugin (an English architect who urged others to "Construct Decoration, Not Decorate Construction"), and further developed by Andrew Jackson Downing (American landscape architect) who expanded them to include asymmetrical design and an explicit sensibility to spatial organization that embraced the totality of indoors and outdoors. Starting with Arthur David's article in 1906, the concept of indoor/outdoor relationship emerges as theme with variations in most of what has been said about the Greenes up to this moment. (See Chapter III, Quintessence).

An authentic Japanese structure, built by Japanese workmen in 1876 on the Fairmount Park site of the Philadelphia Centennial, stood for many years in stunning contrast to its surrounding Americana, "revealing us as, architecturally speaking, the most savage of nations," wrote C. Matlock Price in 1916. Tantalizing wisps of the Orient in the decorative arts had made their way from the continent to Britain and even to the eastern American seaboard, but the opening of Japan's ports by Admiral Perry in 1853 was politically significant, and, in addition, permitted scholarly travel and religious proselyting. It awakened a tremendous curiosity about Japanese art and architecture. (One hundred years later, the trend seems reversed — Japan is coming to our shores for lumber, Oriental religions have permeated the fabric of Western life, and the pervasive appreciation of the whole Oriental aesthetic has enabled a synthesis in art and architecture in southern California that contradicts the platitude, "East is East . . .").

Boston became the hub of the American fascination with the Orient; from this center of culture went Ralph Adams Cram, Ernest Fenollosa and Edward S. Morse to Japan, and back to its museums came some of the finest Japanese treasures. Clay Lancaster[4] lists eight principles defining the differences between Western and Far Eastern architecture that reveal compatibility with the pioneering efforts to bring a civilizing order into a "savage" taste in art and architecture: lightness, volume, simplicity, horizontality, forthright exposure of materials, integration of structures and environment, and the architect as a craftsman. These principles, as well as Eastern philosophy, were topics of conversation in gracious Boston parlors while the Greenes were there.

After their two-year course at MIT, Charles and Henry Greene began their professional work in Boston. Although there were several variations of both authentic Japanese buildings and adaptations of them in the central eastern seaboard, the design sensitivity they demonstrated later (between 1903 and 1912[5]) could have had only an initial response during this Boston period. The Phoenix Villa at the Columbia Exposition of 1893 in Chicago, the Japanese gate in San Francisco's Exposition of 1894 in Golden Gate Park, the

4

Bentz Oriental Art Shop in Pasadena, and the itinerant bookseller proffering Morse's JAPANESE HOMES AND THEIR SURROUNDINGS stimulated a later response. From 1903 on, the work of Greene and Greene took on its highly personal character, those not-to-be-duplicated forms, that *something* that set it apart from all the others, writes L. Morgan Yost. "So I would know he was not entirely original, he [Charles Greene] asked me if I would like to see that old book. He took it from the shelf, turned almost automatically to the page and remarked sadly that he had never gotten to Japan. . . ."[6] Most artists and travelers were impressed by the Japanese temple architecture. Morse, almost alone, sketched the soon-to-vanish domestic architecture. The impact of Japanese architecture was by way of the West Coast.

Initiated by the exhortations of John Ruskin, Thomas Carlyle and William Morris in the mid-1800s, the explosion of originality coming at the close of the century — Art Nouveau, Jugend-Styl, Secessionist, Craftsman — was characterized by a denial of classical, historicized forms and a solid resistance to what Reyner Banham, the English architectural historian, calls THE Machine. Approving mainly of the Medieval, because it relied upon a handcraft ethic, Ruskin, Carlyle, and the William Morris School promoted what amounted to a new morality, which combined art and socialism in Britain; this translated on American shores to a force more earnest and democratic.

The Craftsman, a monthly magazine, published from 1901 to 1916 in New York, sponsored an approach to total home design which was part symbolic — the great roof, anchoring the house to the earth — and part style — a more demo-cratic house plan, which allowed the cook a share of the sun, expanded the living room and squeezed the parlor into a manly den. Gustav Stickley, the editor, emphasized that "merely to make things by hand implies no advance." Then he chides those whose enthusiasm for the revival of handicrafts has caused the equal sin of making by hand things for which there is no need, saying that without necessity there can be no living art: "The time is ripe for the birth in this country of a national art . . . that shall express the strongly individual characteristics of the American people . . ."[7] The proliferation of popular home magazines, such as *House Beautiful*, around the turn of the century encouraged these individual characteristics.

The first popular modern furniture in the United States, the simple Craftsman style, was designed by Gustav Stickley to blend into "sincere" settings. It was appropriate with handsplit shingles, exposed beams, and boulder fireplaces in the wide-open California of sun and informality at the turn of the century. Although Stickley furnishings were sometimes scorned as "a veritable sea of mud and mustard," they are now sought in old garages, coast to coast, refinished, museumed, and priced as Art, not furniture. The furniture and accessories designed by Greene and Greene are coveted and cherished even more, and have always been highly regarded.

To assume that sliding doors, total room design (including piano case*), analogous color schemes, adaptations of Oriental art motifs and structures**, and use of indigenous materials***[8] were innovations of the Greenes is to do them a disservice; these effects predate the Greenes, some by more than one hundred years (Jefferson used sliding doors in Monticello), and demonstrate, instead, the Greenes' knowledge of architectural history and their awareness of their own creative period.

This creative period spilled across the continent to the last architectural frontier, resulting in what James Marston Fitch calls a "unique demography." The well-to-do and educated, detached from familiar European roots, were, on the West Coast, brought face to face with the unfamiliar in a genial climate and landscape. The total environment, physical and philosophical, welcomed innovation. The symbols of the liberality of this elite are the movements they sponsored — national parks, birth control, a fresh-air hygiene, Oriental missions, and universities. These were the clients who commissioned the California Bungalow, a western version of that "most generous, gentle form, the shingle house."

It is easier to say what the bungalow is *not* than what it is; a popular elastic term, it stands for the best, as in the Greenes' Crow-Crocker house, or the worst of imitations: the latter were strung like square beads up and down the streets of southern California, foresquare to the street, and could be called the first tract prototype. Growing out of the eastern cottage tradition, the bungalow made new and definite contributions in its informality, its use of common, natural materials, and the relative simplicity of its framing. In 1906, *Country Life in America* "attributes the low cost of the bungalow to its single story, which (1) eliminates construction expense of a stairway, (2) makes external decoration unnecessary, the low form being pleasing in itself, (3) cuts down on vertical plumbing extensions, (4) requires little hall space, (5) keeps framing at a minimum,

(6) avoids heat waste up the stairwell, and (7) calls for plain interior trim."[9]

In the best of bungalows, style was secondary to planning, and if one can see past the quirky roofs, the bouldered porch supports, the pseudo-Swiss, Spanish or Japanese affectations, the contribution that remains is the easy flow of indoors/outdoors. Although A. Page Brown built the first bungalow near San Francisco in 1895, Charles and Henry Greene worked variations between 1903 and 1912 establishing a level of innovation and quality that leads many writers to award them the distinction of creators of the California Bungalow. This is an achievement comparable to Frank Lloyd Wright's Prairie House.

No literature on architecture today ignores the "messianic genius" of Frank Lloyd Wright. This was not true during the period of 1895-1915, when he and the Greenes had parallel careers half a continent apart; then each was a regional phenomenon. Comparisons that clarify similarities and differences are helpful as long as they are considered within the context of their time. The similarities were: elaborate renderings, often in color; a trained woman artist in the office; a fireproof design system; furniture as an integral part of the total design; a specialist cabinetmaker entrusted with implementing designs; offices in their home community as well as in a metropolis; house designs published in current homemaking magazines; speculative houses, as well as those planned for individual clients; features such as inglenooks, porte cocheres, sleeping porches, elaborate designs in tile around fireplaces, billiard rooms, wide eaves, windows in multiples, and use of materials in their natural form.

For a thorough, lucid investigation of differences in structure between designs of Frank Lloyd Wright and those of Greene and Greene, read William H. Jordy;[10] for an important experience common to both architects, with very different reactions and results, read Grant Manson's revealing descriptions of the Japanese buildings at the 1893 Chicago Exposition;[11] for an overview, read Stephen Jacobs, "California Contemporaries of Frank Lloyd Wright, 1885-1915."[12]

Twelve months of gardens, gentle treeless hills, the tarnished golds of sycamores and brilliant sun — California. The extract from Charles Greene's "California Home Making" (see Chapter III, Quintessence) reveals the architects' response to the well-promoted community of Pasadena soon after their arrival in 1893. Harwell Hamilton Harris' essay on "Regionalism"[13] reminds us that architecture "cannot exist without buildings, and buildings cannot exist without clients, and clients cannot be pushed or led very far in advance of the head of the procession — at least not in sufficient numbers to create a movement broad enough to be called a regional expression. The state of mind that distinguished the region made [the Greenes'] work possible." And the clients: "To be expressed," Mr. Harris continues, "an idea must be built. To be built, it must be particularized, localized, set within a region. And what are important are not the limitations of the region but the resources of the region." Rarely do the resources of compatible philosophies, a generous pocketbook and an unhampered year in which to build "an Idea" converge as they did in The Gamble House, or in what Robert Judson Clark, editor of *The Arts and Crafts Movement in America: 1876-1917* calls the "four great houses" — Gamble, Pratt, Blacker, and Thorsen.

The evolution of the Greene and Greene style is as intriguing as these great successes — the Tichenor house, in which the Oriental sympathy first flares (1904); the Cordelia Culbertson house, more Chinese, restrained (1912); the James house near Carmel, a western Tintagel (1918), fissured like the cliff brow it surmounts. But the welcome of the Blacker Keeper's house is like a low Japanese bow, and the aerie in Charles Greene's own home on Arroyo Terrace, and the entrance bridge to the Nathan Bentz house, (formerly a treasure of Oriental art) are a lasting tug on the heart. Burchard and Bush-Brown in THE ARCHITECTURE OF AMERICA do not credit the Greenes with the creation of a style. They did not leave an enormous legacy; however, it was an enduring one, "the finest and most genuine form California regionalism has achieved."[14]

The year 1914 marks what Vincent Scully calls The Moment of Passage "between two very different Americas, the old one with a few roots in the earth, tough and inventive, the new one fully industrialized, purse-proud and insecure."[15] Stuart Bailey, in a Master's Thesis on The Gamble House, noted in 1954 that the Greenes, and the Craftsman movement from which they sprang, looked backward in terms of building techniques, rather than forward. Another research paper in the Greene and Greene Library, by Miriam Golbert, concludes that "because they had not put a structurally simplified house back into the hands of builders, copy, degeneration, and deterioration of work had to follow." Henry Greene explains, "It was the flurry of interest in the superficial Spanish architecture that forced discontinuance of our work."[16] But in Reyner Banham's more universal view, "the precious vessel of handicraft aesthetics . . . was dropped . . . . Between Futurist dynamism and Academic caution the theory and design of the architecture of the First Machine Age were evolved."[17]

In 1927, Thomas Tallmadge doomed the architecture of originality and of freedom from traditional styles by asking, "What is the culture and genius of America? It is European!" Nine years later, he calls Louis Sullivan not "Champion of the Lost Cause," but "Parent and Prophet." This is the hinge time. There is also a shift in attitude back toward the vernacular after an uneasy fifteen-year courtship of the International Style. John Kouwenhouven in MADE IN AMERICA predicts the "increasing awareness that the best work in American architecture grows directly out of the democratic and technological necessities which force us to think in terms of economy, simplification, and fitness for human purposes."[18] Familiar — and quite adjustable to the cleansing qualities of a newer functionalism.

Early in the 1930s Americans looked again at the Shaker barns, the Cape Cod cottages, the rambling western ranch houses and acknowledged their straightforward use of material and adaptation to climate and topography. Suddenly the redwood houses of the Berkeley Hills looked amazingly fresh, a flexible native style that could become American Modern without a serious break. When, in 1946, an eminent architectural critic characterized West Coast buildings as examples of "Bay Region Style," contrasting them favorably with the International Style, this reference to the Greenes' work conjured up the proverbial "tea-with-lemon" tempest. "If someone was in search of a regional style, he missed it by about 500 miles. Such a style can only be credited to Greene and Greene," said Jean Murray Bangs.[19] "If 'human' is considered identical with redwood all over the place, or if it is considered identical with imperfection and imprecision, I am against it; also, if it is considered identical with camouflaging architecture with planting, with nature, with romantic subsidies . . ." countered Marcel Breuer in the Museum of Modern Art symposium on 'What is Happening to Modern Architecture' in 1948. The echoes of this lively coast-to-coast debate resulted in a reevaluation that hailed Maybeck and the Greenes as pioneers of modern (small m) architecture, alerting critics to a new generation of architects practicing in California who did work that clearly belonged to a similar tradition of structuralism in redwood (William Wurster, Harwell Hamilton Harris, John Galen Howard).

Since World War II, modern architecture has come back to the ideals of individuality and articulation, and to a renewed interest in history. In 1953, Esther McCoy used the word craftsman (small c) in referring to the Greenes in Roots of Contemporary Architecture; in 1966, in THE FORGOTTEN REBEL (i.e., Stickley) John Crosby Freeman wrote of "currently overlooked Arts and Crafts" (capital C); and in 1973, The Gamble House was billed as one of the finest examples of The Craftsman Movement.

Harold Kirker writes in CALIFORNIA'S ARCHITECTURAL FRONTIER, "In the nineteenth century California developed no new important building techniques, initiated no major architectural trends, advanced no significant architectural theories . . . . The work of Charles and Henry Greene represents an end — not a beginning — in the long tradition of creative experimentation with wood forms that started in the 1840s as an American reaction to the late eighteenth-century English picturesque classicism." He adds that the flowering of the bungalow style was an unconscious synthesis of the entire course of California architecture in the 19th century. Coming after the disappearance of the frontier, "it is the first indigenous domestic architecture in California."[20]

John Entenza, in his Foreword to FIVE CALIFORNIA ARCHITECTS, suggests that the enormous fertility of western American architecture will continue to "enrich, infuriate and enliven" both the professional and nonprofessional world of building; southern California builds the trend-setting house, starting with the California Bungalow by Greene and Greene.

NOTES

[1] Philip Johnson, at Yale University, in Preface to ARCHITECTURE, AMBITION, AND AMERICANS — Wayne Andrews, 1964.

[2] Ralph Adams Cram, in Preface to AMERICAN COUNTRY HOUSES OF TODAY, Paul Wenzel and Maurice Krakow, compilers, p. ii. Architectural Publishing Co., New York, 1913.

[3] William H. Jordy, AMERICAN BUILDINGS AND THEIR ARCHITECTS, 3, pp. 221-223. Doubleday, New York, 1972.

[4] Clay Lancaster, "Metaphysical Beliefs and Architectural Principles: A Study of Contrasts between Those of the West and Far East," The Journal of Aesthetics and Art Criticism 14, March 1956, pp. 287-303.

[5] The period between the Bandini House (1903) and the Cordelia Culbertson House (1912) is considered their most creative period. William R. Current (see Reading List, Books), suggests that there were three stages of Japanese influence in the Greenes' career: first, the decorative — Boston and the Massachusetts Institute of Technology environment; second, the structural — Bandini, Irwin and Gamble Houses; third, philosophical, when C. S. Greene moved to Carmel, to study Buddhism, to write, to carve, and (incidentally) to do less architecture.

[6] "Greene and Greene of Pasadena," Journal of the American Institute of Architecture 14:3, September 1950, p. 123.

[7] Gustav Stickley, "The Use and Abuse of Machinery, and Its Relation to the Arts and Crafts," The Craftsman 11, November 1906, pp. 202-207.

[8] *C.F.A. Voysey, H.M. Baillie Scott.
**E.W. Godwin, J.M. Whistler
***A.G. Schweinfurth, Charles Augustus Keeler

[9] October, pp. 627, 640.

[10] AMERICAN BUILDINGS AND THEIR ARCHITECTS, 3, pp. 217-245. Doubleday, New York, 1972.

[11] FRANK LLOYD WRIGHT TO 1910, pp. 34-38. Reinhold, New York, 1958.

[12] In PROBLEMS OF THE 19TH AND 20TH CENTURIES, Studies in Western Art, Vol. IV, pp. 34 ff. Princeton University Press, Princeton, New Jersey, 1963.

[13] Harwell Hamilton Harris: a collection of his writings and buildings, "Regionalism and Nationalism," pp. 25-33. Student Publications of the School of Design, P.O. Box 5273, Raleigh, North Carolina.

[14] P. 230. Little, Brown & Co., Boston, 1961.

[15] MODERN ARCHITECTURE, p. 29. George Braziller, New York, 1961.

[16] Henry Greene, quoted by Esther McCoy, "Roots of California Contemporary Architecture," Arts and Architecture, 73, October 1956, p. [4].

[17] Reyner Banham, THEORY AND DESIGN IN THE FIRST MACHINE AGE, Introduction, p. 12. Praeger Publishers, New York, 1972.

[18] John Kouwenhoven, THE ARTS IN MODERN AMERICAN CIVILIZATION, pp. 209, 210, 233. W. W. Norton & Co., New York, 1967. (New title).

[19] "Greene and Greene," The Architectural Forum, October 1948, p. 81.

[20] Pp. xiii, 129. Peregrine-Smith, Salt Lake City, Utah, 1973.

Quintessence

Hosmer House, Pasadena, 1896

THE BRAVE INTENTIONS of a particular period are often swallowed by the larger currents of the time. It is the happy task of a later intention to stir the old dust and discover what may still be relevant.

Many architects write. Louis Sullivan's words may have stirred more men than his buildings — 'form follows function' stays in the ears. Frank Lloyd Wright's giant talent was supported, always, by writing. Charles and Henry Greene were not known as writers; their words are as regional as the structures they designed, and one does not contradict the other. Read the poetic description of the mission arch form; then find it in the arches of the Nathan Bentz house, the window of the later James House — different functions, different materials, and always the site as arbiter.

Arthur, Ashbee, Stickley and Wight, knowledgeable contemporaries, bring a gentle judgment that mediates between that first decade and our seventh, today. It has all been said; one of the uses of history is to delight.

Dr. Hull's home and office later became the home and shop of Grace Nicholson. Her first great interest was the Southwest Indians and their crafts; later she became fascinated with the Orient and when her collection outgrew these buildings, the Chinese-style building that first housed the Pasadena Art Institute and is now the Pacificulture-Asia Museum was erected in 1924 on the site.

"At first of course, we worked from the outside in, selecting our special model, Cotswold, Tudor, etc., . . . translating it into inexpensive terms, and then fitting into its obdurate shell the requisite accommodations — not without some violence done both to style and convenience, in the process." Ralph Adams Cram, Preface to: AMERICAN COUNTRY HOUSES OF TODAY, 1913, Wenzel and Krakow.

Dr. George Hull, House and Office, Pasadena, 1895

"The main stream of architectural innovation flowed westward from earlier beginnings in the northeastern states and the region around Chicago. This continuity of older creative efforts was matched by a rebellion against an increasingly dominant academic architecture . . ."

Frederick Gutheim, 1857-1957: ONE HUNDRED YEARS OF ARCHITECTURE IN AMERICA.

Fay House, Pasadena, 1898

Note the "poppy roof" on the tower form, the academic Palladian window on the third floor, and the pierced openings in the foundation wall — very much like those in the wall of The Gamble House side terrace.

All Saints Rectory, 1902

Metilde Phillips House, Pasadena, 1902

The steep roof, diamond pane windows and half-octagon tower of this small house reflects an English cottage heritage.

The Old Art of California

"THE OLD ART of California — that of the Mission fathers — is old enough to be romantic and mysterious enough, too. Study it and you will find a deeper meaning than books tell of or sun-dried bricks and plaster show. Then, too, those old monks came from a climate not unlike this. They built after their own fashion, and their knowledge of climate and habits of life, were bred in the bone. Therefore, giving heed to these necessary and effective qualities there is good and just reason why we should study their works. The same spirit that made possible for this little band of men to accomplish so much may again produce something as good. We of California are not pessimistic. In truth and love these men believed they were doing God's will. No wonder that the work that they have left is beautiful. Simple as it is, and rude, it has something that money cannot buy or skill conciliate. It runs in every line, turns in every arch and hangs like an incense in dim cathedral light. This little band of men, so full of inspiration, so sure of success, could not fail — they did not fail. So far as they were concerned these men triumphed over fate, and, incidentally, we have mission buildings. . . . Consciously or unconsciously we admire the things that are true to themselves and we do not want San Gabriel for a church, or a home, or a hotel — but in itself, as the expression of its own time and place and life, it is beautiful."

Charles Sumner Greene, "California Home Making," *Tournament of Roses* edition, New Years Day, 1905, n.p.

The Hollister House

"THE HOLLISTER HOUSE in Hollywood is a striking example of simplicity and good taste. Set back from the street sufficiently to get a good stretch of lawn in front of the house, the breadth of the whole composition is emphasized by the treatment of the approach to the front entrance. What most people would have done would have been to bring the front walk straight down to the street, thus cutting the expanse of lawn in two and marring the unity of the whole composition. [The walk was run parallel to the house, close to it, from the drive on the left.] In studying the front and side elevations of this house, one instinctively feels the presence of the inner court shown in another illustration. This court is the garden and outdoor living-room, and emphasized the effect of the climatic conditions of California upon the general development of bungalow plans."

Arthur Kelly, "California Bungalows," *Country Life in America*, May 1914, p. 42.

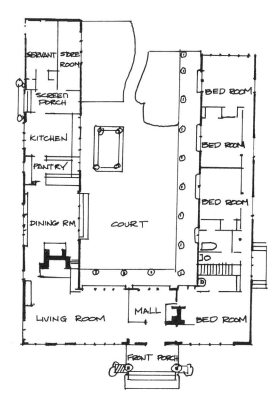

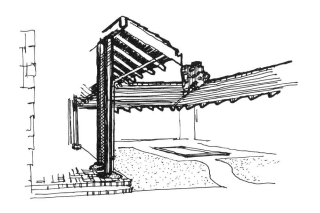

Hollister House, Hollywood, 1904, plan, front elevation, rear patio, details

Charles Sumner Greene on Bungalows

". . . PASADENA is fortunate in having so many beautiful bungalows. The term is stretched to include anything of a house with a long simple roof line. Only the people who have visited India may appreciate the dictionary meaning of the word bungalow, i.e., a Bengalese house. One may often see pictures in the current magazines of California bungalows and much might be said in their praise. It is not so much what one does as how one does it. . . . California prides itself on being up-to-date, perhaps too much, but what a possibility lies in the plasticity of such a mind. No wonder we have experiments, sometimes startling, but often they lead to new and better thoughts. That is the reason why our houses are interesting . . . . The public is in the end the benefactor. So we need not fear experiments . . . .

"As it is, we are not lacking in examples of artistic houses. For the better side of California building we must look to the medium cost houses. Here there is great range and adaptiveness. Wood is the principal building material of the country as yet . . . small houses with all or nearly all rooms on one floor, seem to fill the needs of very many people. To leave out the stairs not only saves expense but adds to convenience as well. To arrange a large living room with entrance direct from the street is not so popular as it once was . . . There is a slight tendency to design for the privacy of the family, though the English idea of the house is not in vogue . . . . The foundation laid in nature's own color and form . . . a rough shake roof toned to the mountains beyond . . . the stone paved terrace . . .

bright with flowers . . . . Furnace fires have ceased to be a necessity but the hearth is not forgotten. One may enter almost anywhere for doors and windows are nearly alike."

Charles Sumner Greene on Gardens

"VOLUMES MIGHT BE WRITTEN about the possibilities of gardens for California . . . . A garden is something planted for the use of man and in order that it may serve its purpose it must be planned . . . . There is much being written about gardens now . . . fine gardens are like fine pictures, only it may take longer to paint them with nature's brush . . . it is not the money we spend, but it is the great want that will be satisfied that finds expression in the beautiful . . . . There are few places in the world that offer so many possibilities without disadvantages to the lover of gardens.

"Pasadena with all of its wonderful possibilities is much behind in her gardens. A lawn with a palm tree in the center may cover the barrenness of the dust, but suppose instead of a backyard we were to arrange an arbor leading at the side to a secluded spot sheltered but not gloomy, where one may leave one's book or work and take it up again at will. Where one could look out into the bright sunlight on groups of flowers, and where one may hear the tinkle of water and see the birds drink. Where the shapely branches of tree or bush cast their lacy shadows fitly across a winding path. . . ."

Charles Sumner Greene, "California Home Making," *Tournament of Roses* edition, New Years Day, 1905, n.p.

Tichenor House, Long Beach, 1904, west view

The Tichenor House

copper chimney top

front gate

"THE TICHENOR HOUSE . . . seems like the utmost limits to which Japanese architecture could be stretched, and still meet American requirements . . . so eloquent that one is tempted to believe that Greene and Greene must have studied the [Japanese] architecture on its native soil. . . . The various materials used in this house are quite along Japanese lines, although each by itself is a well-known one. The half timber work with brick filling is not uncommon, and yet because of the extreme roughness with which the bricks are used, it gives the effect of a new material . . . nor is tile unusual on the roof . . . the brackets and the balustrade are very simply handled in a way thoroughly Japanese, but with a cleverness that is clearly due to the architects and not to the source." The Tichenor Oriental garden was complete with pool, pergola, rocks and specimen plants.

Aymar Embury II, ONE HUNDRED COUNTRY HOUSES, 1909.

The Houses of Messrs. Greene & Greene

".... WE ARE AWARE that the American bungalow derives more of its characteristics from Japanese models than it does from buildings erected in tropical countries ... their houses are open and airy even in winter, and there is no attempt to plan them in the way that we Americans do. ... The climate of California, being both warm and dry, is peculiarly adapted to a low, spacious, airy house of light frame construction.... The California bungalow, consequently, both as a matter of design and as a matter of plan, has about it a certain practical and aesthetic tendency. Its whole purpose is to minimize the distinction which exists between being inside and outside of four walls. The rooms of such a building should consequently be spacious, they should not be shut off any more than is necessary one from another, and they should be finished in wood simply designed and stained so as to keep so far as possible its natural texture and hue. The exterior, on the other hand, should not be made to count very strongly in the landscape. It should sink, so far as possible, its architectural individuality and tend to disappear in its natural background. Its color, consequently, no matter whether it is shingled or clapboarded, should be low in key and should correspond to that of the natural wood. Its most prominent architectural member will inevitably be its roof, because it will combine a considerable area with an inconsiderable height, and such a roof must have sharp projections and cast heavy shadows, not only for the practical purpose of shading windows and piazzas, but for the aesthetic one of making sharp contrasts in line and shade to compensate for the moderation of color. Its aesthetic character will necessarily be wholly picturesque, and it should be both surrounded by trees and covered, so far as is convenient, with vines .... The houses are highly successful, largely because they so frankly meet the economic, domestic and practical conditions which they are intended to satisfy. All of their chief characteristics — their lowness, their big overhanging roofs, their shingled or clapboarded walls, the absence of architectural ornament, the mixture which they afford of simple means with, in some instances, almost a spectacular effect — all of these characteristics can be traced to some good reason in the actual purpose which this sort of house is intended to meet. Of course, in addition thereto Messrs. Greene & Greene must be credited with a happy and unusual gift for architectural design. Their work is genuinely original ....

"They are prone both in their chimney-breasts and in their foundations to build their walls of large heavy boulders, which are ugly in themselves, and are entirely out of keeping with their surroundings and with the service they perform. When used in a chimney-breast, the effect of such heavy masonry is to make everything else in the room seem trivial .... Their methods of design are not so well adapted to large as to small houses.

"The bungalow is most completely and happily fulfilled in the houses of Messrs. Greene & Greene, which we publish herewith."

Arthur C. David, "An Architect of Bungalows in California," *Architectural Record*, October 1906, pp. 305-315.

Henry Green House, Vancouver, 1904

The Henry Green for whom this house was designed was no relation to Charles and Henry Greene. The English half-timber idiom, popular in the Vancouver area, resembles designs by Samuel Maclure, a prominent architect of Victoria whose career parallels the Greenes' in time, quality of construction and influence. The roof is shingled, exterior walls are of plaster.

17

Biography—Charles Sumner Greene

"CHARLES SUMNER GREENE. A leader in his kind of work . . . the Pasadena architect was born October 12, 1868, in Cincinnati, Ohio. His father, T. Sumner Greene, M.D., physician specializing in nose and throat diseases, also a native of that city, was descended from the same stock as General Nathaniel Greene, of Revolutionary fame. His mother, Lelia A. Greene, *nee* Mather, is descended from Rev. Cotton Mather . . . .

"Charles Sumner Greene received his primary education in the public schools of St. Louis, Missouri, and afterwards took the course at the manual training school of Washington University. In 1889 he was sent to Boston to enter the Massachusetts Institute of Technology. After finishing his course there, he began to work with a Boston firm of architects [Winslow and Weatherall]. He remained in that city several years and was connected with a number of noted men of the profession, among them H. Langford Warren, R. Clipston Sturgis . . . .

"In 1891 Dr. Greene came to California for the benefit of his wife's health, and two years later he induced his two sons . . . to settle here. . . . In partnership with his brother, Mr. Greene opened a modest little office in Pasadena and began to practice his profession. In 1901 the office was moved to Los Angeles, but he still continued to be called the Pasadena architect.

"In February of this same year he was married to Miss Alice Gordon White, of Pasadena, formerly of England. One month later they set sail for London, where Mr. Greene spent some time in studying the later art movements. Before returning home he visited France and Italy. A new inspiration, gathered from the broadening influence of travel, was at once felt and soon brought success. The sympathy he so long sought began at last to make it possible to realize some measure of his ideal in house building for the home. It is this great vital theme that concerns the welfare and happiness of the nation. To him it is the one great interest . . . .

"In 1901 Mr. Greene built his own house on Arroyo Terrace, where one may get one of the finest views in Pasadena. Subsequently, he designed most of the houses in that locality, which has been called "Little Switzerland," with, however, more readiness than propriety. And whether it is for sight of the village or the view, it is certain that no appreciative tourist considers his itinerary complete without this little circuit. [Greene Walk 1].

"Mr. Greene's influence on the domestic architecture of Southern California is plainly to be seen and to those who may appreciate his work, it appeals mainly through its frank simplicity and its great originality."

James Miller Guinn, A HISTORY OF CALIFORNIA AND AN EXTENDED HISTORY OF ITS SOUTHERN COAST COUNTIES. LOS ANGELES: HISTORIC RECORD, 1907, pp. 540-543.

The Pratt House

"The finest Greene and Greene bungalow of the next few years is the Charles Pratt house (1909) on Foothill Road at Ojai, a low, crescent-shaped timber construction, of which only a part is two-storied. The interplay of angles and casually placed planes show the ingenuity of the architects. They have achieved here a synthesis of house and landscaping unequaled elsewhere in America. The central room is a living hall, entered from a terrace of free form, several curved steps above the motor court."

Clay Lancaster, "The American Bungalow," reprint from *The Art Bulletin*, September 1958.

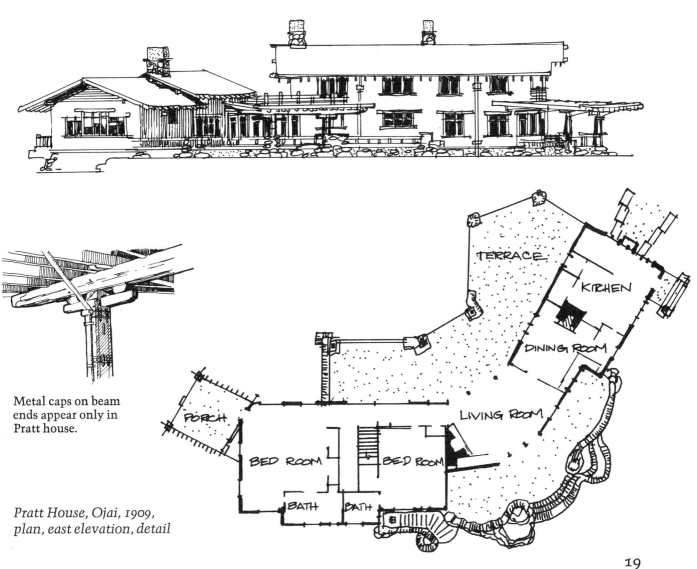

Metal caps on beam ends appear only in Pratt house.

Pratt House, Ojai, 1909, plan, east elevation, detail

"Let Us Begin . . ."

"I AM AN AMERICAN. I want to know the American people of today and the things of today. It is my earnest endeavor to understand the lives of men and women; then perhaps I may be able to express their needs architecturally. I seek till I find what is truly useful and then I try to make it beautiful. I belive that this cannot be done by copying old works, no matter how beautiful they may seem to us now. When confronted with the actual facts, I have not found the man or woman who would choose to live in the architectural junk of ages gone by. The Romans made Rome and the Americans — well! — they are making America. Who could live in a house of two hundred years ago and be happy if we had to conform to all the conditions of today? How in the name of reason, then, can we copy things two thousand years old? Is the Paris opera house built onto the front of a railway station or a Greek temple plastered over the entrance to an office building good art? One is apt to seize the fact for the principle today and ignore the very lesson time should teach. The old things are good, they are noble in their place; then let our perverted fingers leave them there.

"Let us begin all over again. We have got to have bricks and stone and wood and plaster; common, homely, cheap materials, every one of them. Leave them as they are — stone for stone, brick for brick, wood for wood, plaster for plaster. Why are they not better so? Why disguise them? Thought and care are all that we need, for skill we have. The noblest work of art is to make these common things beautiful for man."

Charles Sumner Greene, quoted in: James Miller Guinn, A HISTORY OF CALIFORNIA AND AN EXTENDED HISTORY OF ITS SOUTHERN COAST COUNTIES, LOS ANGELES: HISTORIC RECORD, 1907, pp. 540-543.

For the Prospective Builder

"IN THE BEGINNING there are three great things the prospective builder should know by heart.

First — Good work costs much more than poor imitation or factory products. There is no honest way to get something for nothing.

Second — No house, however expensive, can be a success unless you, the owners, give the matter time and thought enough to know what you want it for. By success, I mean all things necessary to your comfort and happiness in the life you are obliged to lead.

Third — You must employ someone who is broad enough to understand and sympathize with you and your needs and yet has the ability to put them into shape from the artist's point of view.

"The style of a house should be as far as possible determined by four conditions:

First — Climate

Second — Environment

Third — Kinds of material available

Fourth -- Habits and tastes, i.e., life of the owner

"The intelligence of the owner as well as the ability of the architect and skill of the contractor limit the perfection of the result."

Charles Sumner Greene, "Bungalows," *The Western Architect*, 12, July 1908, pp. 3-5.

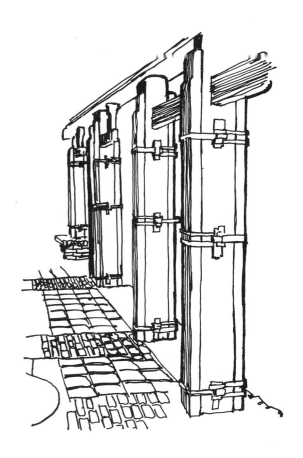

Thorsen House, Berkeley, 1909
West front foundations; rear terrace and supports

The Thorsen House

"GREENE AND GREENE HOUSES build up gradually from the ground. The Greenes gave grave attention to the foundation. How the house joins the ground has proved embarrassing to most architects. Few have sought a solution; most are satisfied with a disguise, and one not in the realm of building. The usual disguise is foundation planting. . . . Greene and Greene houses meet the ground in transitional stages. Fieldstone, clinker brick, with brick or concrete cap, lead the house into the earth, to become a natural part of it. . . .

"To arrive at the appropriate is a slow process. It takes time, it takes deep concern; it takes something of greatness. And these the Greenes had."

Esther McCoy, "Notes on Greene and Greene," *Arts and Architecture*, 70, July 1953, pp. 27,38.

21

Charles Sumner Greene on
Greene & Greene Designs

"THERE IS A SUGGESTIVENESS in the word bungalow that makes it interesting. Just now it is a popular catch word — all the more because few of us have seen a real one. There is play for the imagination. We have never called our houses bungalows but we cannot shake off the appellation however removed it may be from a semblance of anything Anglo-Indian.

"The wondrous climate of California and the freedom of the life one may lead here have much to do with the development of the style of house illustrated in this issue. . . .

"As to environment, — in such a place as Pasadena with people in easy circumstances and willing enough, it is plain to see how the California architect of "bungalows" must be what he is — for better or worse — a man dependent upon his own power of expression rather than of rigid custom.

"Low roofs but with broad eaves and perfectly ventilated roof spaces are required . . . terrace walls to give the needed privacy to those who would enjoy the view from out of doors . . . these walls also protect from the dust of street traffic. The character of these walls was determined upon after a study of the general conditions. A style that admits of freedom from convention will obviously lend itself to this sort of thing. Natural rocks built in with bricks may offend the eye that admits only one cult, or perhaps the eye that is unaccustomed to it may wonder; but time and place should fitly determine a custom of men, — the walls I believe serve the purpose for which

they were intended. For the rest, the exterior of these houses are of common enough materials obtained in local market, but so put together as to warrant their durability and with such ordinary ingenuity and grace as the architects were capable of.

"In regard to the practical advantages of casement windows, we have found that a long row of narrow windows gives the best results because one may open any number to gain perfect ventilation without unpleasant draughts. They can be made weather tight when hung to swing in or out. We drape them with single heavy curtains that exclude the sun, — usually one curtain to each sash to slide upon a pole specially designed so that they may be drawn to one side if desired.

"Leaded glass is sometimes used and it is very effective where it seems to fill a real need.

"Doors should be interesting in themselves and not merely holes of entrance and exit. This need not make them too conspicuous. For this kind of work batten doors seem very appropriate. . . .

"Hardwood floors seem to fill all of the demands of this kind of house. Rugs, either Oriental or specially designed are most appropriate. Still there are some domestic hand wove fabrics that are good.

"The fireplace should be a thing of use. It is to be deplored that it has at present degenerated into a design for the pressed brick manufacturer. However, steam and furnace may have displaced it, the fireplace from the aesthetic point of view will always be necessary. . . . A real fireplace does heat and does not smoke. If it does this much it will be appreciated, but to be a real joy it must appeal to our love of the beautiful. The materials have little to do with the success. It may be only a sheltered nook with a cozy seat put together with a little thought and love in the effort; perhaps the pleasure of giving others pleasure sawed and hammered and pegged into it all with the passion that makes beauty grow. . . . [There follow descriptions of the houses on Arroyo Terrace. See Greene Walk 1].

"It may be interesting to know that Arroyo Terrace is not a straight street but is an irregular curve from one end to the other, thus no house can be set at a right angle to the street, — neither are any of the houses in line, but by careful study this has been compensated for and does not strike the observer as anything unusual."

Charles Sumner Greene, "Bungalows," *The Western Architect*, 12, July 1908, pp. 3-5.

The Gamble House

"The vitality of the visual experience depends not only on the dynamics with which structure is immediately sensed as an assemblage, but . . . in the way in which the parts are adjusted to one another . . . roofs are structurally fragmented and appear as parasols . . . porches seem suspended as cages within the shadow of the roof . . . the interior bears out the character promised outside . . . ."

William H. Jordy, AMERICAN BUILDINGS AND THEIR ARCHITECTS, Vol. 3, p. 249.

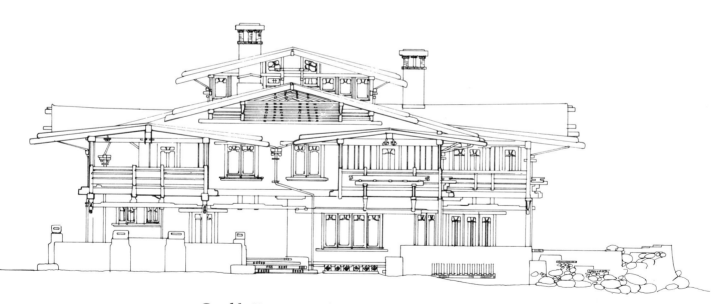

Gamble House, Pasadena, 1909, north elevation

"Pasadena Portico of Paradise": Materials

". . . INDIGENOUS . . . a style of building which every native understands . . . local tradition . . . always results from using only local materials, never from using imported materials. . . .

"Mr. Greene has used California Redwood, the white cedar of Oregon, the granite boulders of the Arroyo and even the brick of Pasadena, poor as it is. Almost without exception he has imported no material and he has put great thought into the handling of these local materials. It is the developments which he made with local wood and stone which have made it possible for others to successfully follow his lead. . . .

"The development of the new mode of building in reinforced concrete has grown in Southern California with leaps and bounds. There is good reason for this local development. We have material at our doors everywhere which makes cement. We have sand and gravel by the square mile. It is a certainty that when the day of wood is gone by, the day of concrete and its various developments will be here to remain. . . . The permanent building of the future in Pasadena is going to be much lighter in color than now, is going to approach more nearly the color of buildings under similar skies.

". . . We shall never have an architecture which does not show our racial origin, but someday someone will conventionalize, simplify and set the standard for a white building of the south which fits California as Charles Greene has so beautifully conventionalized and adapted another type of building to another phase of our requirements."

"Pasadena Portico of Paradise": Style

". . . TWO DISTINCT architectural trends seem to be working with us side by side. One represents the call of the north, of the traditions and precedents which the northern emigre brought with him, the other is the call of the south with its bluer sky and clean-cut shadows, backed by another tradition, a tradition which came to California from a similar climate in southern Europe, from Spain and the Mediterranean up by way of Mexico. The architectural traditions of the Mission Fathers are everywhere in evidence.

"There are many cities of equal size with Pasadena which may contain more individual buildings of high architectural merit than does Pasadena, but there is no city in the world which has as high an average of architectural standing, which makes as good a first impression upon the newcomer as does Pasadena. . . .

"Although the work of two Pasadena architects . . . the Messrs. Greene, does not always follow this trend toward the traditions of the south, it has had, nevertheless, the most remarkable and the most beneficial influence on Pasadena building traditions. They have gone to Switzerland and to Japan for their motives. Perched on the edge of the Arroyo the buildings of Little Switzerland have become a place of pilgrimage. The momentum which they have started has spread like wildfire. Few of their imitators have equaled them."

By a Los Angeles Architect, "Pasadena Portico of Paradise," *Rose Tournament and Carnival Number,* 1911, n.p.

Nathan Bentz House, Santa Barbara, 1911, southwest elevation

Nathan Bentz House

Nathan Bentz, Oriental art connoisseur, opened the Bentz Shop in Santa Barbara in 1891. He is the brother of John Bentz of Pasadena and Philip Bentz of San Francisco, both proprietors of Bentz Shops also specializing in Oriental art. This home in the Santa Barbara hills is set midway between Olive and Prospect Streets. In a great garden floor gallery the owner displayed his inspiring collection of porcelains, jade, rugs, and carvings. Both roof and walls were covered in split shakes, "11" to weather." The foundations and arches were clinker brick. Note Oriental lilt in small roof over a second floor window, corner knee braces and slender windows in the attic. Entry bridge is on upper level (north side), and there are stone torii gates on both the Olive St. and Prospect St. sides.

Emissary from English Arts and Crafts

"I THINK C. Sumner Greene's work beautiful; among the best there is in this country. Like Lloyd Wright the spell of Japan is on him, he feels the beauty and makes magic out of the horizontal line, but there is in his work more tenderness, more subtlety, more self-effacement than in Wright's work. It is more refined and has more repose. Perhaps it loses in strength, perhaps it is California that speaks rather than Illinois . . . .

"He . . . took us to his workshops where they were making without exception the best and most characteristic furniture I have seen in this country. There were beautiful cabinets and chairs of walnut and lignum-vitae, exquisite dowelling and pegging, and in all a supreme feeling for the material, quite up to the best of our English craftsmanship . . . .

"Here things were really alive . . . . and the 'Arts and Crafts' that all the others were screaming and hustling about, are here actually being produced by a young architect, this quiet, dreamy, nervous, tenacious little man, fighting single-handed until recently against tremendous odds."

C. R. Ashbee, MEMOIRS, 3, Notes, Los Angeles, 1909, p. 106. See also: Dr. Robert Winter, "American Sheaves from C. R. Ashbee," *SAH Journal*, November 1971, pp. 317-322.

Mortimer Fleishhacker Residence, Woodside, 1911

The Mortimer Fleishhacker Estate

CHARLES GREENE directed the development of the extensive grounds of this large English country-style house over a period beginning in 1911. This commission was largely responsible for his eventually moving north from Pasadena. The house, of brick construction with a gunite skin, has a rolling shingle roof. The interiors are of smooth and beautifully molded plaster. Charles did some furniture for this home, more baroque than his previous designs.

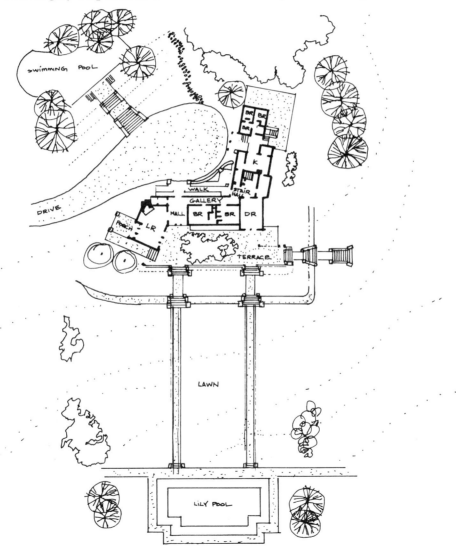

California's Contribution

"THE VALUE OF WESTERN ARCHITECTURE, locally and to the nation at large, and its widening influence upon homebuilding all over the country are facts not to be estimated lightly . . . . America is writing her own architectural history, and writing it with no uncertain hand . . . the West has for some time been recording on the fair page of the Pacific Slope . . . [and] the significance of this Western accomplishment arises chiefly from the sincerity of spirit in which it is being undertaken. The type of home that abounds today in California . . . is no architectural pose, no temporary style. It is a vital product of the time, place and people, with roots deep in geographical and human needs. It has a definite relation to the kind of climate and soil, the habits of the people and their ways of looking at civilization and nature.

It is equally rich in historic traditions and in provision for present needs. Based on the old Mission forms, which in their turn drew inspiration from the ideals of Spaniard and Moor, modern California architecture has nevertheless made those traditions servants, not masters.

"In every instance, the dominant note of their [i.e., Greene and Greene's] work is sincerity — and that, after all, is the thing that is going to make California's architecture a vital record in the chronicle of the nation, and help push forward the art of home-building toward our great democratic ideal."

Gustav Stickley, "Domestic Architecture in the West—California's Contribution to a National Architecture: Its Significance and Beauty as Shown in the Work of Greene and Greene, Architects," *The Craftsman*, 22, August 1912, pp. 532, 547.

Kew House, San Diego, 1913

The Kew House

The Kew residence is another in the English country house style, similar to the Ware and Fleishhacker, designed in the 1911-1913 period. It has a rolling shingle roof and shingle infill above the first floor level. The lower aggregate wall surface is coarsened with increasingly larger flat stones near the ground.

The California Style

"THE CALIFORNIA STYLE has Messrs. Greene and Greene and Mr. Mulgardt to set it forth, and they do it justice, but one must see the real and revolutionary thing in its native haunts of Berkeley and Pasadena to appreciate it in all its varied charm and striking beauty. Where it came from, Heaven alone knows, but we are glad it arrived, for it gives a new zest to life, a new object for admiration. There are things in it Japanese; things that are Scandinavian; things that hint at Sikhim, Bhutan, and the fastness of Tibet, and yet it all hangs together, it is beautiful, it is contemporary, and for some reason or other it seems to fit California. Structurally it is a blessing; only too often the exigencies of our assumed precedents lead us into the wide and easy road of structural duplicity, but in this sort of thing there is only an honesty that is sometimes brazen. It is a wooden style, built woodenly, and it has the force and the integrity of Japanese architecture. Added to this is the elusive element of charm that comes only from the personality of the creator, and charm in a degree hardly matched in other modern work."

Preface by Ralph Adams Cram, in Paul Wenzel and Maurice Krakow, compilers, AMERICAN COUNTRY HOUSES OF TODAY, 1913, p. v.

"Building Bungalows Is Not a Crime"

"SIXTEEN YEARS seems a very brief space of time when one thinks of the building of Rome, but in these sixteen years, the growth of California has been phenomenal, almost unbelievable. Our Rome has not been built yet, it is true, but we have covered the ground. Beneath all this haste of speculation and the sordidness of commercialism, there is an impulse of wholesome enthusiasm born with the sight of the soil and the sun of this wonderful land. One is forced to believe that this will continue and that in the end, it must triumph over exotic tradition and produce a style of architecture best suited to its own endless possibilities . . . we live in a sun-warmed ether near the blush of roses and we know it . . . we may not be expected to be quite rational, but the realization of one thing has come to us, that life in California may be appropriately different from that in Kamchatka, or Kokomo, or Boston, where they are always right. . . . We would like to have them think well of us . . . but we can't prevent building bungalows.

"Building bungalows is not a crime in itself; it is the quality of the product that may justify the practice or condemn it . . . . Between the automobile mania and the bungalow bias, there seems to be a psychic affinity. The spirit that animates the one makes the other possible . . . they seem to be the expression of the same need, to be free from the commonplace of convention. . . .

"The perfect bungalow should be designed to fit the needs of a particular owner. A house built to sell is like to a slop-shop coat; it will cover most any man's back . . . the bungalow architect must study carefully the conditions of the problem and the personality of the owner. . . . It is easy to make pictures . . . once the design of a bungalow is fixed by means of a picture, it is very hard to change it . . . books are worse than architects' pictures . . . they offer the ready-made in the evolution of a progressive art, they may help to arouse interest and must cease to be used when the enlightenment of the people transcends this method of furnishing plans. . . . The value of design is far from being appreciated in California, but the seed is sown. . . . A spring is no higher than its source. . . ."

Charles Sumner Greene, "Impressions of Some Bungalows and Gardens," *The Architect*, 10, December 1915, pp. 251, 252, 278.

Towards City Planning

"HOW FAR THE ARCHITECT, so called, may have been responsible for our public taste in building is a matter of conjecture. . . . As creatures of environment few of us are able to thwart the thrust of immediate pressure. Some of us have our little dreams that come nearly true, paper castles that find embodiment . . . others there are who find the world a place too noisy in which to dream, so set their muscles tense with doing. . . .

"An architect is a builder employing the process art . . . art, either as an individual or a community expression, is a conscious act. Art is a premeditated, correlating arrangement of the qualities of things . . . an intent and an act of recording that intent. . . . The hope of the immediate revival of the art process in building seems to point to the awakening interest in city planning. . . . Both the citizens and the planners will profit by an awakened public consciousness that in the end must become conscience. . . ."

Charles Sumner Greene, "Architecture as a Fine Art," *The Architect*, 13, April 1917, pp. 215, 218, 219, 221.

Charles Greene, Architect, in Carmel

" 'ORDINARILY, when plans are made for a house, after careful study they are practically final, and the specifications minutely exact. These are turned over to a contractor who by contract produces the completed product. Whether he does the work by percentage or a stated sum doesn't matter, he directs the work. Now the James house [1918] was not built that way. The architect hired the men and directed the work personally; except for the plumbing, electric wiring, and tiling, there were no contracts.

" 'Here is the difference; prevailing custom is a system of administration by recorded instruction; mine is not *any* system, but personal direction on the job. The first is fixed, the second is elastic, yielding to contingencies, open to inspiration.' "

Charles Sumner Greene, quoted in: Elmer Gray, "Some Country House Architecture in the Far West," *Architectural Record*, October 1922, pp. 310, 315.

The James House

"THE HOUSE APPEARS to me as though by some species of spiritual affinity it had alighted upon the rocky bluff and stayed there . . . or else was born upon the rock itself. . . . The material of which it is constructed is practically the same rock as that upon which it is built. The long narrow pieces of this stone have been cut into hori- zontal fissures by very deeply struck joints of un- even width. This gives the same general worn-by- age appearance as that of the cliffs. The color aspect of the stonework is saved from sameness by a tile roof of a delightfully faded old rose color — and the tiles are distributed around in just the right proportions, some on top of the chimneys and other bits elsewhere, so as to form a proper color balance. They are not laid in geometrical lines either vertically or horizontally. Nine archi- tects out of ten would have laid them that way,

James House, Carmel, 1918-1930

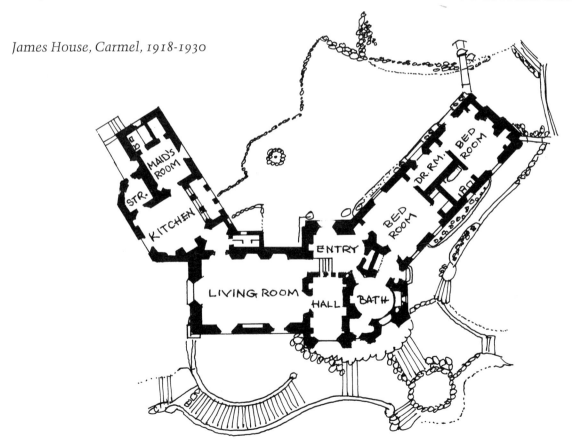

but this is an instance where not only were rules forgotten but where the architect went out of his way to violate them. The ridge lines roll up and down with delightful waywardness, and the vertical lines of the tile appear and disappear as if their usual course has been intentionally broken.

James House, Carmel, 1918-1930

The way some of the main lines of the building grow out of the rock and huge boulders upon which they are built, their foundations often beginning many feet below and gradually working upward in sympathetic conjunction with the native cliff rock, has been managed so skillfully that it is impossible in some cases to tell where the one ends and the other begins. This kind of work is not architecture as architecture is now commonly known — it savors of a more plastic art, of the building of a home in thorough keeping with its rugged site."

Elmer Grey, "Some Country House Architecture in the Far West," *Architectural Record*, October 1922, p. 310.

Rational and Constructive Woodwork

"GREENE AND GREENE introduced a style of roof covering, a continuous composition of woven material of a very light color which reflected the rays of the sun and made it possible to build roofs of less pitch than when shingles or tiles are used. [A 1908 newspaper article referred to this material as malthoid.] This reduced the height of roofs, though this feature has proven to be practicable only in the Southern California climate. But it helped to accent the horizontal character of buildings . . . .

"There is no scarcity of clay for brick manufacture, and in this there are always some . . . deformed bricks. It occurred to Charles Sumner Greene some years ago, that these would help to decorate basement and retaining walls, by building the good ends into them and letting the bad ones stick out to secure color, light and shade by interspacing them with cobblestones and boulders so as to make the walls really beautiful. He was one . . . of the first reformers among the architects of the coast, and had the satisfaction of getting good results by working with the men on his buildings until they also became artists in cobblestones, boulders and discarded bricks. Then he finished his job by planting vines at their base, and left the later development to Nature."

Peter B. Wight, "Residential Architecture in Southern California," *Western Architect* 29, September 1920, p. 94; and "California Bungalows," *Western Architect* 27, October 1918, p. 97.

Biography of Henry M. Greene

"HENRY M. GREENE attended the public schools of St. Louis, Missouri, and the famous St. Louis Manual Training School, famous because it was the first of its kind in America and was the embodiment of the idea of Calvin M. Woodward, of the Civil Engineering Department of Washington University, St. Louis. The manual training, introduced and fathered by Professor Woodward, was an epoch in educational work and was later introduced in the high schools all over the United States. The course was three years, and in 1888, in a class of fifty students, Mr. Greene was graduated with honorable mention. In the fall of the same year, he entered the Massachusetts Institute of Technology with the class of 1892, to take a special course in architecture. His great-grandfather, Thomas W. Sumner, was an architect. After his course there, Mr. Greene spent some time in Boston, working in the office of Chamberlain & Austin, Edward R. Benton (one of McKim, Mead & White's men), and for the firm of Shepley, Rutan & Coolidge. In the fall of 1892 he came to Pasadena, California, and began the active work of his profession here in 1894 in association with his brother, C. Sumner Greene, under the firm name of Greene & Greene. . . .

"During the continuance of the above firm nearly 400 buildings [see Introduction to Structures List] in California, mostly residences, were planned and superintended. The firm made a study of climatic conditions and designed the work so as to take advantage of them. The ideals which the firm tried consistently to follow were: avoidance of sham and insincerity in design and construction; striving to embody the owner's personality and ideas of his needs into a unified whole which was beautiful and at the same time simple, without being bound by traditional style; giving much thought and study to all parts and details, often designing the grounds and interior furnishings as well as the building itself. . . .

"At Rock Island, Illinois, on August 22, 1899, Mr. Greene married Miss Emeline Augusta Dart.

"In political faith Mr. Greene has always been a republican, has served many times on election boards and was a charter member of the widely known Americus Club during the McKinley campaign. At the first call for volunteers for service in the World War, although beyond the age limit, he registered with the Tech Club in Washington. Before many weeks he received a call to supervise the construction of airplane factories, but when the order came he was critically ill with rheumatic fever and was unable to do any work for many months. While convalescing he had to content himself with aiding in the Liberty Loan work and served as captain of a district.

"Mr. Greene is a member of Corona Lodge No. 324, F. & A. M., Pasadena. He is a member also of the American Institute of Architects; the Southern California Chapter of the American Institute of Architects; Pasadena Chamber of Commerce; Engineers of Pasadena; Alumni Associations of St. Louis Manual Training School and Massachusetts Institute of Technology, and of the Red Cross Society, and formerly was a member of the Archaeological Institute of America and active in the Automobile and Twilight Clubs."

John McGroarty, HISTORY OF LOS ANGELES COUNTY, II, American Historical Society, 1923, pp. 220-223.

Henry M. Greene on Design

"... THE WHOLE CONSTRUCTION was carefully thought out and there was a reason for every detail. The idea was to eliminate everything unnecessary, to make the whole as direct and simple as possible, but always with the beautiful in mind as the final goal."

Henry M. Greene, quoted in: Gustav Stickley, "Domestic Architecture in the West — California's Contribution to a National Architecture: Its Significance and Beauty as shown in the Work of Greene and Greene, Architects," *The Craftsman*, 22, August 1912, p. 536.

"WE WERE ABLE to do our best design when we could control the complete landscaping and decorating, as well as the house. This is the only possible way to achieve integration of all three."

Henry M. Greene, quoted in: Esther McCoy, "Who Starts a Style?," *Los Angeles Times*, Home Magazine, July 19, 1953.

" 'IN MY DAY,' said Henry, 'you could proceed to do a job and carry it out completely. We didn't need to have inspections. A craftsman's work was his reputation.'

"He pitied those who lived and worked in what he called this period of transition."

Henry M. Greene, quoted in: Randell Makinson, "Greene and Greene," in Esther McCoy, FIVE CALIFORNIA ARCHITECTS, 1960, p. 146.

The Architect as Artist Recognized

"... IN THE PROVERB 'Exceptions prove the rule' the word 'prove' originally meant 'tests.' Another aphorism: 'A prophet is not without honor save in his own country' is tested and disproved by the brothers Greene, who have lived long enough to be recognized and appreciated by their countrymen and fellow-professionals, in contrast to Sullivan whose recognition during his lifetime was hardly more than the publication of some of his designs by the American Institute of Architects.

"Official recognition of the work of Greene and Greene, a Southern California AIA Chapter Special Certificate of Merit 1948 and a National AIA Citation 1952, were no doubt considered adequate by these modest pioneer architects, supplemented by an increasing flow of published photographs, brochures and articles on their work. They have both gone on to their eternal rewards; Henry Mather Greene in October [2] 1954 and Charles Sumner Greene on June 11, 1957, having had in their mortal years the assurance of a kind of immortality which few achieve, a strong recognizable influence on the work of others and the esteem of their patrons and fellow professionals. But it would be an impossible feat of research and scholarship to appraise fully and adequately their contribution to American architecture from the vulgarization of their bungalow houses by carpenter-builders across the continent to the more basic contributions in freedom of planning and design and the essence of Far Eastern architecture and decoration distilled through their sensitive souls and talented hands, long before the current more direct and obvious influence in contemporary work.

"Charles Sumner Greene and his brother epitomize and aid in perpetuating the ideal which we are always in danger of losing — the architect as artist."

Walter A. Taylor, "Charles Sumner Greene," *Journal of the American Institute of Architects*, November 1957, p. 402.

ANNO DOMINI MCMLII

ARCHITECTS MUCH HONORED IN YOUR HOMELAND FOR GREAT CONTRIBUTIONS TO DESIGN. SENSITIVE AND KNOWING BUILDERS WHO REFLECTED WITH GRACE AND CRAFTSMANSHIP EMERGING VALUES IN MODERN LIVING IN THE WESTERN STATES. FORMULATORS OF A NEW AND NATIVE ARCHITECTURE

THE AMERICAN INSTITUTE OF ARCHITECTS

NOW HAILS AND HONORS YOU

CHARLES SUMNER GREENE

AND

HENRY MATHER GREENE

FOR YOUR CONTRIBUTIONS TO THE DESIGN OF THE AMERICAN HOME. YOUR GIFTS HAVE NOW MULTIPLIED AND SPREAD TO ALL PARTS OF THE NATION. AND ARE RECOGNIZED THROUGHOUT THE WORLD. INFLUENCING AND IMPROVING THE DESIGN OF SMALL AS WELL AS GREAT HOUSES. YOU ENRICH THE LIVES OF THE PEOPLE. YOU HAVE MADE THE NAME OF CALIFORNIA SYNONYMOUS WITH SIMPLER. FREER AND MORE ABUNDANT LIVING. YOU HAVE HELPED SHAPE OUR DISTINCTIVELY NATIONAL ARCHITECTURE. AND IN GIVING TANGIBLE FORM TO THE IDEALS OF OUR PEOPLE. YOUR NAMES WILL BE FOREVER REMEMBERED AMONG THE GREAT CREATIVE AMERICANS

SECRETARY   PRESIDENT

IV   List of Structures

A CERTAIN LOOSENESS in the use of the attribution Greene and Greene may have enhanced the ambience of Pasadena and worked to the advantage of sales promotion, but it has disadvantaged the Greenes and obfuscated any sure knowledge of what was, indeed, designed by these two architects.

Not all that looks Greene and Greene is: some that does is not! There are statements by the two architects deploring the discouraging proliferation of copies of their work; there may well be structures not yet located. How to determine . . . ? Memories are unreliable, city directories and publications may be in error, tax records are meager for these early years, and "authorities" have sometimes found their previous 'facts' modified by newer evidence.

Job numbers were assigned to each client contact: these number designations were usually retained whether the contact remains a project (i.e., projected, not built), or was completed. There may be many job numbers assigned to one client over a period of time, for a residence, for a garage, for a later addition, or perhaps another residence. A substantial addition — garage, studio — constitutes an entry on this list. Even small commissions — a piece of furniture, an alteration to an existing structure (not necessarily one the Greenes designed), or a sketch — were given separate job numbers. The job numbers for Greene and Greene go as high as 547, covering the years 1893 to 1951. Charles Sumner Greene lived and worked in Carmel after 1916 and the firm publicly ceased to exist in 1922. A previous estimate of the number of "Greene and Greenes" (inferring houses) was 350. Within the last few years this total has been trimmed to 300, and the author's estimate is about half this number.

In the handwritten autobiographical sketch of 1907, Charles Greene says we have built "several small business blocks," "several hundreds of dwelling houses." Even if the original job book is available, it is difficult to determine what was projected and what was actually completed. There are "Specifications for a California House" by Greene and Greene, including spec sheets and blueprints; there are plans labeled "G. L. Stimson," a prolific builder in Pasadena contemporary with the Greenes; there are linen drawings for the Pasadena Security Investment Company; there are drawings for a combination of eclectic features different from those considered typical of the Greenes; there are houses ostensibly by other architects or builders which the Greene and Greene experts can only puzzle over. These puzzles may some day be solved to explain the discrepancy between Charles Greene's phrase "several hundreds of dwelling houses" and the number of houses documented so far as being authentic Greene and Greenes.

Because small commissions that can be moved (furniture), and alterations and/or additions (which may be visible only interiorly), and projects (which are archival in nature), are not readily available to the public, they are *not* included on this Structure List. Any entry on the list has met at least two of the following criteria:

1. Linen drawings and/or blueprints with office identification.

2. City, social, and telephone directory listing, on or near the appropriate date.

3. Photographs in early publications or archives (publications are helpful, not always accurate).

4. Job numbers.

5. Documentary information, i.e., letters, journals, obituaries, firsthand reports of the period, area histories, etc.

6. Official tax and county records.

Authorities date structures in various ways. The method used in this book is realistic rather than precise. For instance, if drawings are dated February 1908, and a photo of that year shows a building partly constructed, but no City Directory listing appears until 1910, a date of 1909 seems realistic (e.g., The Gamble House). Hyphenated names mean ownership is ambiguous or tightly sequential. All the evidence is not in. . . .

Occasionally houses believed to be demolished have, in fact, been moved. Entries followed by D (demolished) and a date contribute an important mute dimension.

Key:

GW1 — Greene Walk 1 (or Greene Walk 2, 3, etc.).

Drwg. — Sketch, detail or plot plan.

P — Plan (layout of rooms).

D — Demolished.

M — Moved.

* Information credit, Randell Makinson.

Numbers — Pages on which reference to house occurs.

V   Greene Walks

THE FIRST Greene Walk started spontaneously one moist Sunday in November, 1966. Since finding Greene and Greenes is a Pasadena pastime, Gamble House Docents (and husbands), numbering twenty-five this day, were curious, enthusiastic, but only slightly knowledgeable. From 436 South Arroyo Boulevard their route led north onto South Grand Avenue, crossed Colorado Boulevard, curved around Arroyo Terrace to Westmoreland Place, and ended in the kitchen of the Gamble House with hot soup, homemade bread, cheese, and wine. This is approximately the route of Greene Walk 1 in this book. It has been repeated often.

Since that time there have been walks each year, with walkers numbering twenty to sixty-five, including many owners of Greene and Greene houses. Only once did rain curtail the expedition. As more areas were explored and bits of information accumulated, an Area File was begun. It became important to know dates of construction, something of the clients' requirements, details about furnishings, and the names of the present owners. Whatever could be observed from the outside would be enriched by experiencing the inside. This was not always possible. The walks have always been solely a Docent activity. Some further explorations on the part of individual Docents to other cities and libraries led, inevitably, to research that has substantially augmented the Greene and Greene Library and made this book possible. Megs Meriwether has been a welcome and invaluable research arm of Greene Walks preparation for several years. Much of the nonbook material is in the Greene and Greene Library because, as a newly trained Docent in 1969, she modestly volunteered to join the fledgling library committee and be in charge of vertical files. Her activities in behalf of the stated aims of the entire Library have propelled her to many other locations. Under the guidance of Myrtle Clark, a professional librarian and also a Docent, she has taken a course in library procedures and is now in the Docent training program at the Huntington Library. In locating sources for out-of-print publications, and becoming familiar with libraries and research facilities between San Diego and San Francisco, she has uncovered material which has immeasurably enriched the List of Structures, the Greene Walks, the Reading List and the Greene and Greene Library.

To walk is to understand the contribution Greene and Greene structures make to the total context of the community. Some are being lovingly restored and will endure (Bentz, Van Rossem-Neill); others are adapted to new uses (Cole, Pitcairn); life for others, still recognizable as Greene and Greenes (Bolton, Herkimer Arms) is precarious; and at least three will vanish before a freeway as transportation takes precedence over residence (Garfield, Longley, Rowland).

The selective sketches in this section reveal noteworthy architectural details that are easily seen from public access but might be overlooked in a photograph or through architectural innocence. Since these are mostly residences, the privacy of the occupants should be respected and their custodial care appreciated. For an interior view, visit The Gamble House, and for early illustrations, make an appointment to use the Greene and Greene Library.

"System was a relationship of parts — one to the other and to the whole — a relationship of change: change of plane, material, of connections and joinery. An expression of the role and identity of each part."

Randell Makinson, "An Academic Paper: The Gamble House," *The Prairie School Review*, p. 25.

Halsted entrance

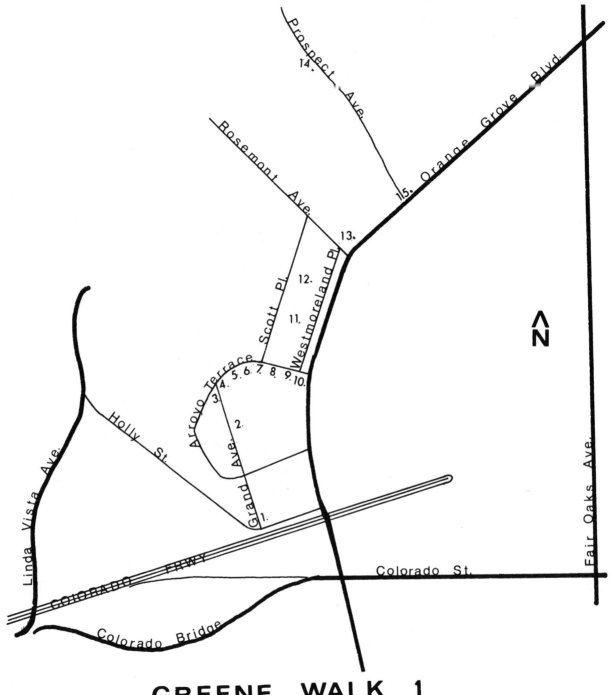

GREENE WALK 1

Halsted, roof elevations

1. HALSTED, 90 North Grand Avenue   1905
As one approaches the intersection of Colorado Boulevard and Orange Grove from the south, the hovering roof elevations of this house are exceptional. It was originally a one-and-a-half-story seven room house with the entrance on the southwest. Greene and Greene did several alterations and additions, including a garage and gardener's cottage, for this owner of the Pasadena Ice Company.

"The individual character of their work . . . was expressed in the bold use of heavy timbers, projecting rafters, broad sloping roof lines and overhanging eaves, extensive masonry walls, stained board and batten siding, and the incorporation of the garden into the total design."

Randell Makinson, "Greene and Greene," FIVE CALIFORNIA ARCHITECTS, by Esther McCoy, p. 103.

2. VAN ROSSEM (No. 2), 210 North Grand
Avenue   1904
A simple, practical two story seven room
house, the second of several residences in this
same area for a loyal client. Obvious later accessories.

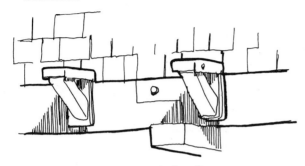

Van Rossem No. 2, window box support

". . . In the application of their design vocabulary
they do not distinguish between indoors and outdoors. Identical spliced and doweled joints are
seen in garden trellis or exposed ceiling beam.
There is no effort to suppress the joint — the
Greenes always emphasize and enhance it. . . ."

Esther McCoy, "Notes on Greene and Greene," *Arts
and Architecture*, 70, July 1953, p. 27 *ff.*

3. CULBERTSON, JAMES, 235 North Grand
Avenue   1903
Originally a two-story English country-style
house of nine rooms, it was furnished with
Stickley pieces. "Typical American Country
Houses," *Country Life in America*, April
1908, states "cost about $10,000." (This was
after some additions.) It was given bay windows in tower form during a 1914 remodeling
and was greatly simplified by major remodel-

ing in 1953 by a Pasadena architectural firm
whose own work reflects a kinship to Greene
and Greene. Note early features (wall, pergola, garages, front door, east end of residence), and later changes (west end of residence, removal of entire second story, incorporation of original stained glass around
front door, etc.). James Culbertson was a
benefactor of the California Institute of
Technology, and a recently demolished
building there bore his name.

". . . One material is never used to hide another.
Each is expressed openly, stating its function, and
each member by its size declares its ability to
carry its load."

Esther McCoy, "Notes on Greene and Greene," *Arts
and Architecture*, 70, July 1953, p. 38.

James Culbertson, base of tower form

James Culbertson, 1903; 1914

James Culbertson, garage supports

51

4. DUNCAN-IRWIN, 240 North Grand Avenue
1901; 1906

A small cottage, built for Katherine Duncan in 1901, was expanded into this considerably larger two-story residence surrounding a very small open court. The Oriental quality of this house is discussed thoroughly by Esther McCoy and Clay Lancaster. "The artistic achievement of the Irwin house is its external composition: the interesting arrangement of closed and open forms, the subtle deviations from orthodox rectangular shapes, the use of soft color harmonies of natural materials, attention to contrasting textural combinations, and an excellence of joinery, which included slight curvatures, especially about the roofs, for aesthetic effect. The design combined a boldness that was not coarse, with a refinement that was in no way effete." (Clay Lancaster, "Some Sources of Greene and Greene," *AIA Journal*, August 1960.)

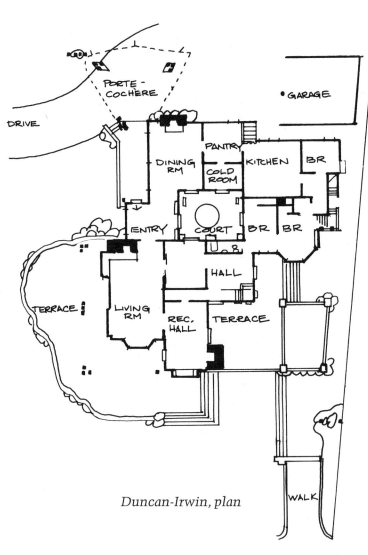

Duncan-Irwin, plan

52

"Above all, it should be noted that the verandas are not mere adjuncts or afterthoughts . . . but major elements, both space-wise and visually, of the whole composition. . . . "

Henry-Russell Hitchcock, ARCHITECTURE: 19th & 20th CENTURIES, p. 266.

Duncan-Irwin, porte cochere support

Duncan-Irwin, three brick pillars, entrance terrace

Duncan-Irwin, west view window

53

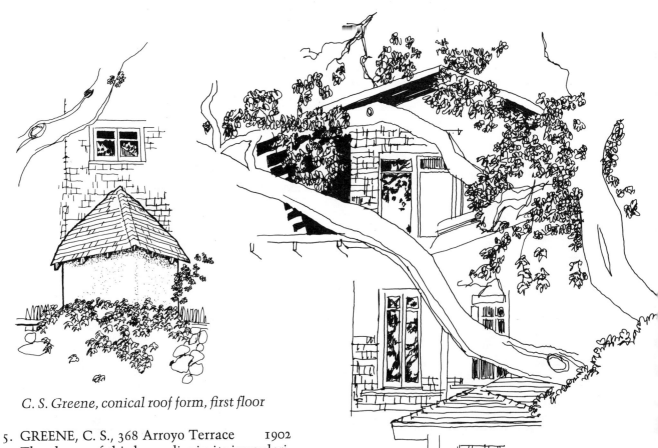

C. S. Greene, conical roof form, first floor

5. GREENE, C. S., 368 Arroyo Terrace   1902
The charm of this house lies in its irregulari-ty, its siting above the edge of what is now Brookside Park, and its construction up into the arms of a spreading oak tree. Here Charles Greene experimented with design concepts and made additions and alterations as the family grew. The garage is a later con-struction; the handsome original doors are stored at present.

C. S. Greene, third story, later addition

Gnarled oak trees, characteristic of the arroyo area, provided inspiration for the design of the magnificent three-section front door, containing Tiffany glass, in The Gamble House.

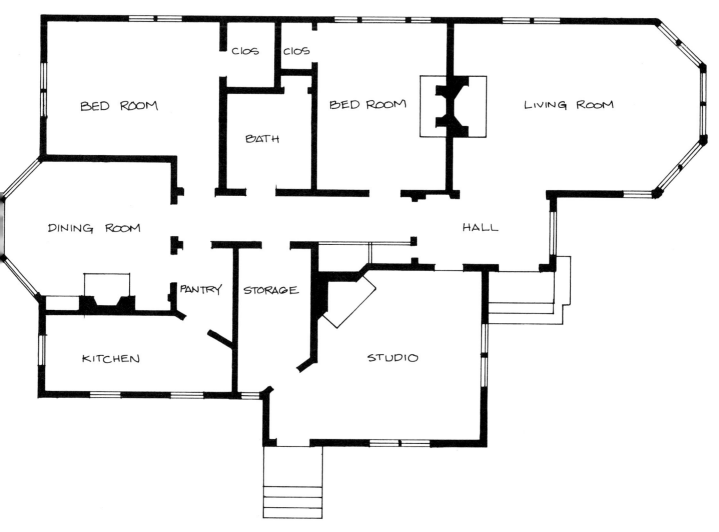

BED ROOM

CLOS CLOS

BED ROOM

LIVING ROOM

BATH

DINING ROOM

HALL

PANTRY STORAGE

KITCHEN

STUDIO

"House for Mrs. Charles Sumner Greene, Pasadena"

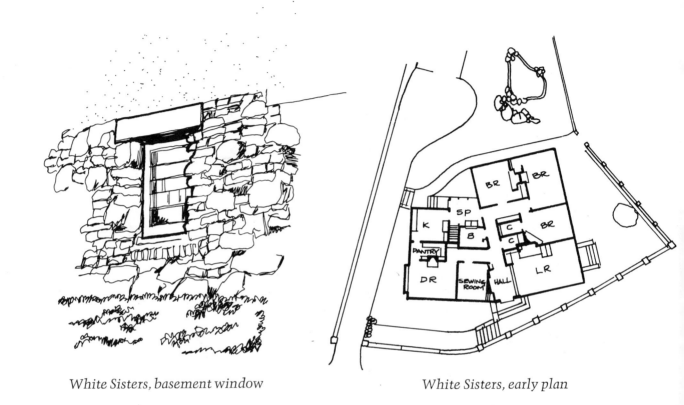

White Sisters, basement window

White Sisters, early plan

6. WHITE SISTERS, 370 Arroyo Terrace 1903
This is probably the Greenes' first bungalow
and was originally covered by cedar shakes
like many others in the area. This house, for
the three sisters of Mrs. Charles S. Greene
(Martha, Violet and Jane) was built concur-
rently with 368 Arroyo Terrace. A rear pergola gate once linked this property with that
of the C. S. Greenes to the west.

7. VAN ROSSEM No. 1—Neill, 400 Arroyo
Terrace   1903
Built for "a certain lady who shall be nameless" (i.e., Van Rossem), this house was added
to and altered by James W. Neill in 1906,
when the clinker brick wall with insets of
Chinese tile was built. Meticulous restoration and furnishing is in progress inside and
out, including removal of exterior plaster and
replacement of shingles, the initial surface.
It appears in illustrations before 1972 as
Neill.

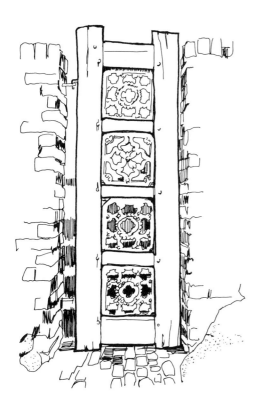

Van Rossem-Neill, gate with tiles

Tiles measure 12″ x 12″ and are shades of rich
green. These are used also in The Gamble House,
Blacker Keeper's torii, Herkimer Arms Apartment House, (now painted white) and others.

Van Rossem-Neill, base of porte cochere support

57

8. HAWKS, 408 Arroyo Terrace   1906
Similar in plan and scale to other residences done by the Greenes in this decade (Porter Bentz, Phillips). The brick and boulder drive and generous porch of this eight room, two-story house are most appropriate in this location. The garage was once single-story. Mr. Hawks was one of the founders and supporters of Polytechnic Elementary School.

"Throughout their work is a clear statement of the Greenes' almost religious belief in the integrity of basic units, in the use of system as a means to the organization of a multiplicity of elements or units...."

Randell Makinson, "An Academic Paper: The Gamble House, *The Prairie School Review*, p. 24.

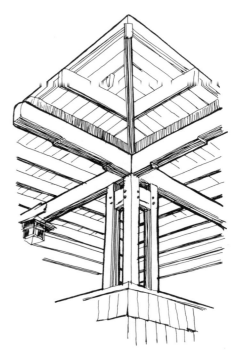

Hawks, underside of porch corner

Hawks, plan

Hawks, side view of front step

58

9. WILLET, 424 Arroyo Terrace   1905
This simple one-story six room shingle bungalow, built for Judge Willet as a rental, was topped by a second story and encased in stucco by a subsequent owner in 1934. Curving walk, terrace and front door, and windows give clues to original state. Alternate typical bungalow plans were published in Wilson's book accompanied by Greene and Greene illustration.

Willet, original frame, one-story structure

"Complete plans and specifications of this house with all necessary interior details, either as shown on this page or reversed, will be furnished for $10."

THE BUNGALOW BOOK — Henry L. Wilson, 1908.

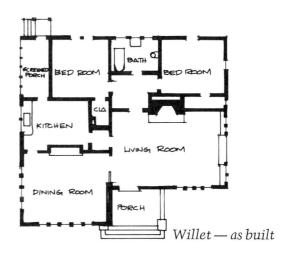

Willet — as built

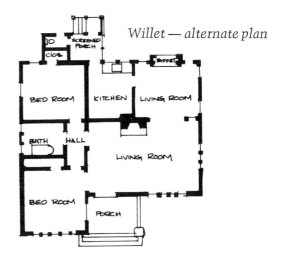

Willet — alternate plan

59

10. RANNEY, 440 Arroyo Terrace   1907

Mary Ranney, who founded Westridge School in 1912, assisted in the design of her own eight-room house while with the firm of Greene and Greene. The sizable addition to the northwest was made in 1912. Most of these lots below the shoulder of the former reservoir are wedge-shaped; this house faces the corner.

The Van Rossem House No. 3 at 223 North Orange Grove Avenue (around the corner) was built in 1906 and demolished in 1955 when its triangular lot was absorbed into the reservoir property, now filled with compatible condominiums. Una Nixon Hopkins, in "A House of Fine Detail . . . ," *The Craftsman*, June 1907, writes in great detail about this house that is "carved up and down like an apple tart." C. S. Greene, in an article entitled "Bungalows" in *Western Architect*, 1908, describes these houses by the Greenes along the curve of Arroyo Terrace, i.e., numbers 4 through 10.

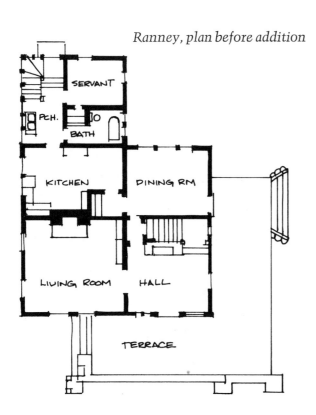

Ranney, plan before addition

Ranney, horizontal beams between first and second floors

60

11. COLE, Formerly No. 2 Westmoreland, now
301 North Orange Grove   1907
The first use of a porte cochere by the
Greenes was on this $26,000 "bungalow."
The massive chimney on the west end of this
commodious house is unique, as is its adaptation to multiple current uses by Neighbor-
hood Church. The firm of Smith and Williams has developed a church campus on
former lots 1, 2, and 3 on private Westmoreland Place that integrates the Cole residence
in a manner that maintains the vocabulary
of woodenness and horizontality, and sensi-
tively spans the decades between 1907 and
1973.

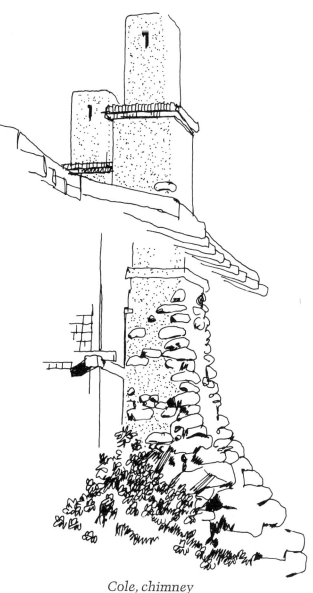

Cole, chimney

"The craftsmanship of Greene and Greene is that of elaboration, albeit the elaboration of essentials and not mere intricacy for its own delightful or tortuous sake. They explode the structure into its opposed components, and then elaborate the opposition . . . ."

William H. Jordy, AMERICAN BUILDINGS AND THEIR ARCHITECTS, 3, p. 229 ff.

Cole, upper balcony, rear

12. GAMBLE, 4 Westmoreland Place   1909
This residence headlines the area and is the latest in time, greatest in size, and finest in detail. Cost; $50,000. Although all of Pasadena is abundantly rich in architectural history, this heritage is most concentrated in Greene Walk 1. (See Table of Contents for complete information about The Gamble House.)

"The strength of Greene and Greene architecture is revealed in its plan; in The Gamble House, e.g., one long closed box to the left of the front door, another exposed open box to the right of the front door, lightly linked by the hall space which is 'open' front and rear.

"On the outside the shingle says 'thin wall, constantly interrupted,' upon which the roof imposes an order, the metaphor of shelter: on the inside one feels as if one is inside a piece of sculpture, akin to the ship-building tradition. The wall surfaces are no longer neutral so the structure becomes the furnishing."

Reyner Banham, Visiting Lecturer, "Craftsman Architecture," for Department of Architecture, University of Southern California, December 11, 1973. Notes by Janann Strand.

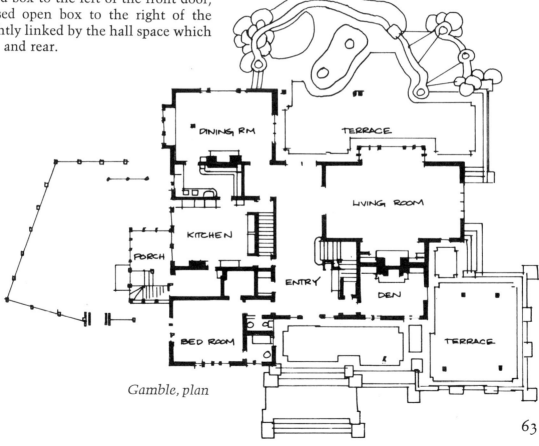

Gamble, plan

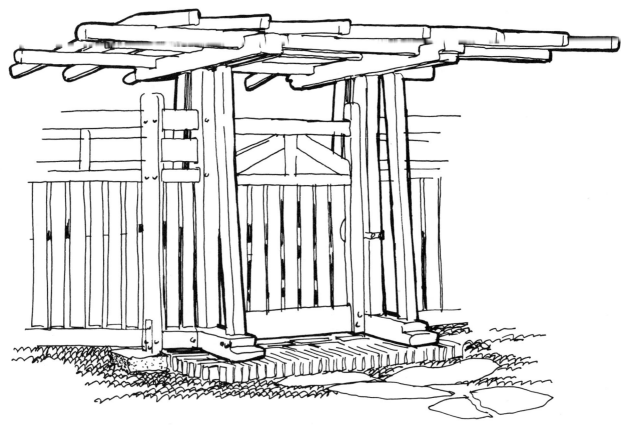

Gamble, kitchen pergola-gate

"Could any two things be linked together more perfectly, each playing into the other's hands than Messrs. Greene & Greene's fragment of a house called "West Gate and Entrance to Kitchen?"

Preface by Ralph Adams Cram, in Wenzel and Krakow, AMERICAN COUNTRY HOUSES OF TODAY, 1913.

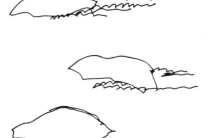

Gamble, garage corner

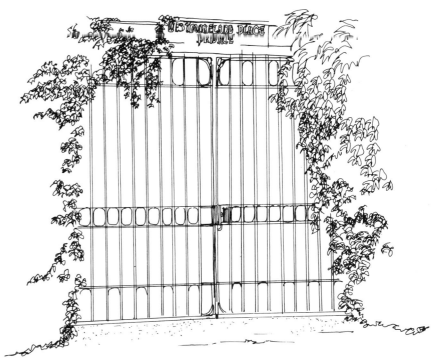

Westmoreland Gate, at Rosemont

13. WESTMORELAND GATE   1913
The elaborate iron gate at the north end of Westmorcland Place at Rosemont, permanently closed, was built in 1913. The earlier post-boulder south portal no longer exists.

14. BENTZ, 657 Prospect Boulevard   1906
The Prospect Tract, in concept and endur-
ance is a hallmark of Pasadena, and the de-
votion with which this particular house has
been restored has inspired a preservation
movement in this city. This residence, designed for the owner of the Bentz Oriental
Shop, is a classic two-story, moderate-sized
eight room shingle house.

Bentz, third-floor vents

A large trellis once extended out from this wall
to the south.

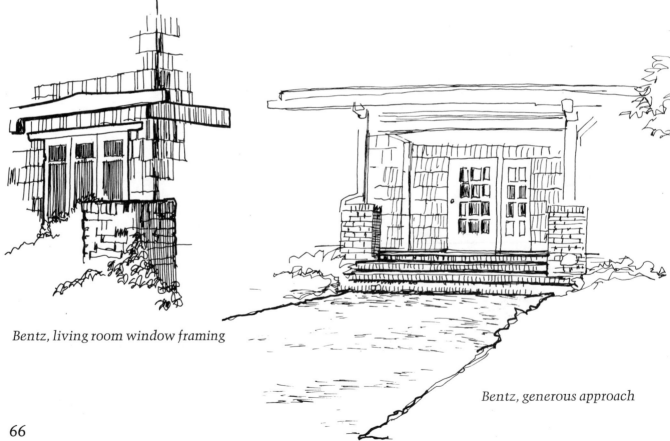

Bentz, living room window framing

Bentz, generous approach

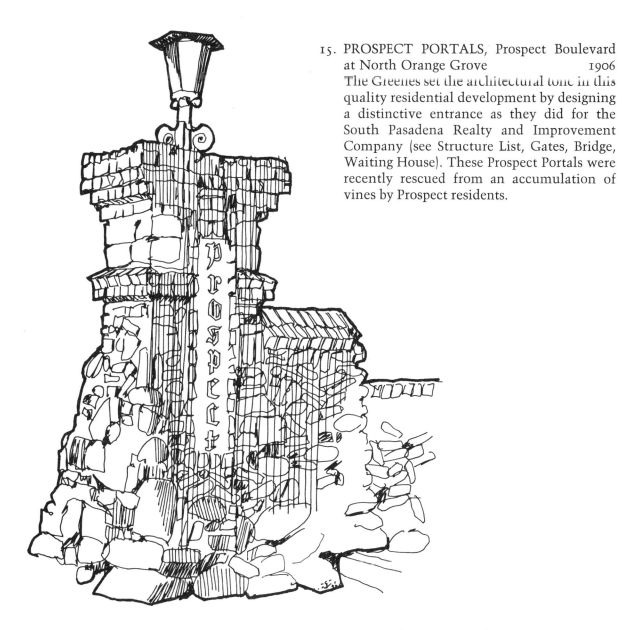

15. PROSPECT PORTALS, Prospect Boulevard
    at North Orange Grove   1906
    The Greenes set the architectural tone in this
    quality residential development by designing
    a distinctive entrance as they did for the
    South Pasadena Realty and Improvement
    Company (see Structure List, Gates, Bridge,
    Waiting House). These Prospect Portals were
    recently rescued from an accumulation of
    vines by Prospect residents.

Prospect Portals

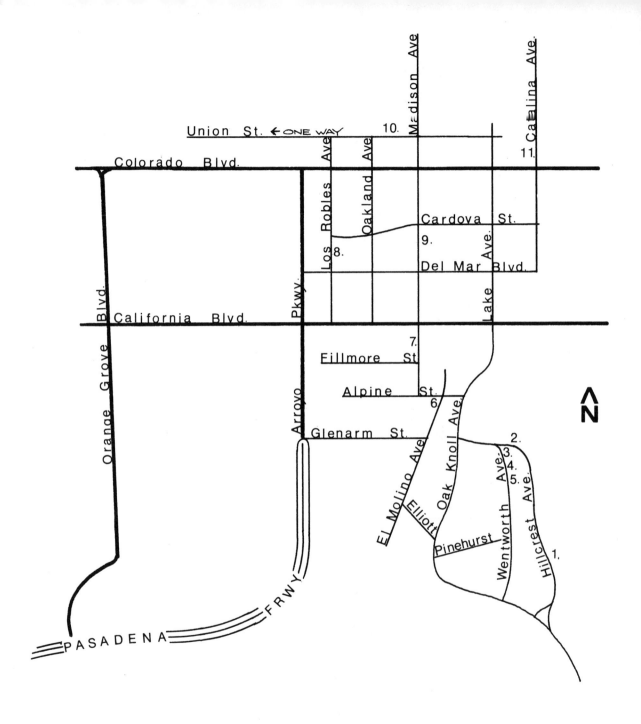

GREENE WALK 2

1. SPINKS, 1344 Hillcrest Avenue   1909
The living room and dining room of this delightful house, which is situated on the far edge of the property, overlook a prominent arroyo. There are second floor hall ceiling windows to allow greater light and ventilation control similar to those in the Crow-Crocker corridor. Careful restoration continues on this residence which cost about $11,000 when built.

"These are the most perfect houses, I believe, that have ever been built. . . . Theirs was not a machine architecture; it was the last beautiful bloom of hand craft. . . ." L. Morgan Yost, "Greene and Greene of Pasadena," *AIA Journal*, September 1950, p. 124.

Spinks, light-vents, third floor

"The positive quality which emerges is that of the skeletal pavilion."

Vincent Scully, THE SHINGLE STYLE, p. 158.

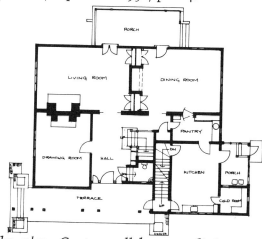

Spinks, plan. Center wall between living room and dining room later removed.

Spinks, eave of front porch

2. CULBERTSON, CORDELIA, 1188 Hillcrest Avenue   1912

Designed for the three sisters of James Culbertson (Greene Walk I), and ultimately the most expensive of all the Pasadena residences, this one demonstrated an early use of gunite for walls that were originally a mellow rusty tan. A two-story rear bedroom wing overlooked extensive lower gardens, no longer existing. The single-level south facade is quite Chinese; this feeling is enhanced by the exceptionally beautiful green tile roof. The large, grassy inner patio opens east and is partially closed by a vine-covered pergola. A centrally located garden room facing onto this patio has a retractable window wall. On the lowest level, below the bedrooms, is a small ballroom with stage, one of many elaborations added by a later owner, F. F. Prentiss; this name is often mentioned in connection with the (former) gardens.

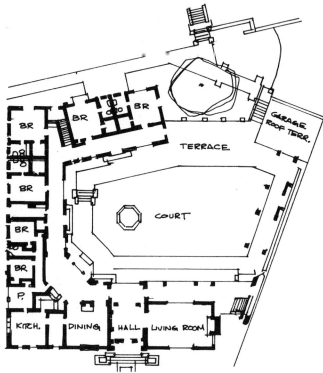

Cordelia Culbertson, plan

Garden room with retractable wall is on the inner corner to the left of the main hall.

Cordelia Culbertson, tile detail, continuous in all walkways and terraces

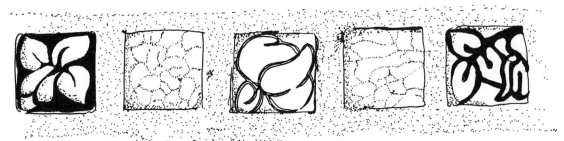

70

Cordelia Culbertson, entrance

"Redwood is easily worked, which facilitated the Greenes' extensive and intricate joinery . . . yet it is strong, elastic and durable enough to stand up under generations of use. It takes the weather well. Termites avoid redwood and it resists rot. It planes evenly and takes a fine soft polish. It is a material as suitable for a beam twelve or sixteen inches square as it is for the finely drawn mullions in a bookcase."

Stuart Wilder Bailey, "The Gamble House, 1908 . . .", 1954, p. 104.

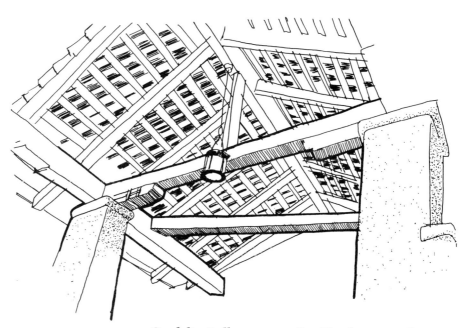

Cordelia Culbertson, underside of porte cochere

3. BLACKER, R. R., 1177 Hillcrest Avenue 1907
One of the largest, most complete and costly residences by the Greenes, built for a lumberman from Chicago, it has been reshingled by its present owner, also in the lumber business. The massive timbers, like those in older Japanese temples, are combined with the interior refinement found in palace architecture, and some of the essential characteristics of domestic construction in the countries of southeast Asia — broad eaves, sub and attic air spaces, and easy openings. The original grounds, landscaped under the direction of Charles Greene, comprised five and a half acres and included a large Oriental pool, stream, pergola, garage, keeper's house and lath houses. There are a lower-level billiard room, porches, verandas, and arbor, insets of Tiffany glass and a very distinctive angled porte cochere. The exquisite furniture made for this house now enriches several homes. The present owners deserve praise for careful preservation and maintenance. This residence has been widely pictured and was shown in a section entitled "Continuity and Rebellion" in an exhibit for the 1957 A I A Centennial. See Frederick Gutheim, 1857-1957: ONE HUNDRED YEARS OF ARCHITECTURE IN AMERICA.

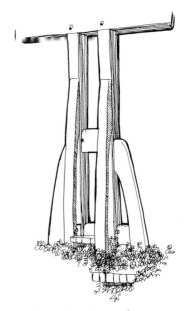

R. R. Blacker, arbor support

R. R. Blacker, entrance seat

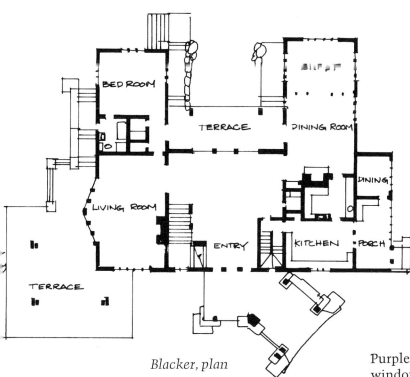

Blacker, plan

R. R. Blacker, stair window

"This plan, in all its essentials, was borrowed from one delineated by Myron Hunt and Elmer Grey for R. R. Blacker . . ."

Clay Lancaster, THE JAPANESE INFLUENCE IN AMERICA. (Credit for this information to Robert Judson Clark. Plan published in *Architectural Record*, October 1906.)

Purple is a dominant color in this stair landing window; several thicknesses of glass are used, which gives a particularly rich effect from the inside.

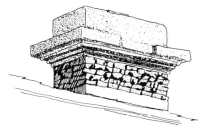

R. R. Blacker, chimney

R. R. Blacker, south end of dining room

73

4. BLACKER, R. R. (Garage), 1200 Wentworth
Avenue   1907
The north/south wing is not by Greene and
Greene but was added to the original garage
to create this residence in the 1940s.

5. BLACKER, R. R. (Keeper's house), 1208
Wentworth Avenue   1907
A central interior wall was removed by the
present owners to expand the living room for
this one-bedroom residence. The entrance
torii gate is new construction: the driveway
torii is original but tile made from a special
mold, shipped from the Philippines, was in-
serted by present owner.

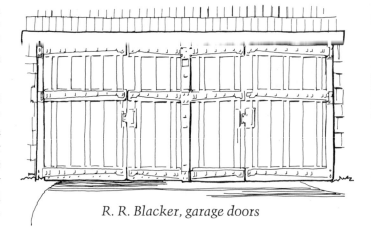

R. R. Blacker, *garage doors*

"In their work we are constantly aware of the
stick, used as a post, as a beam or composing lat-
tice, trellis or truss. We see the stick joined together by notch, dowel or strap; the stick making
the rhythmic pattern and the joints the decorative detail.

We are aware of the board, wide or thin, joints
open or closed, with lap, plain-faced batten or
tongue and groove. We see boarding long and
narrow; boards parallel or criss-crossing in woven
open patterns as in a fence or terrace railing. Or
we see the board short and thin, methodically arranged in a textural pattern of partial overlay, as
in the large expanses of shake-covered walls. . . .

The durability of their structure is in a large
measure due to the fact that they made no effort
to achieve a continuity of line that belies the
multiplicity of the parts beneath it."

Jean Murray Bangs, "Greene and Greene," *The Architectural Forum*, October 1948, p. 85.

R. R. Blacker, Keeper's House, *driveway torii*

74

6. CROW-CROCKER, 979 South El Molino
Avenue   1910
Plans indicate this house was designed for
Dr. S. S. Crow in 1909 and later actually built
for Edward S. Crocker in 1910. The property
included a guest house (See Structure List,
separate entry, 1912), and extensive lawns
north to the corner of Alpine Street. The U-
shaped plan provides a narrow patio with
skylit interior corridor along one side. The
chimney and roof elevations are quite refined

on this $10,000 residence, designed by Henry
Greene while Charles was traveling in Europe.

"Greene & Greene design embodied one of the
basic principles of democratic architecture. It
made no class distinction between the large and
the small house. The whole weight of its influence went to break down the difference between
'palace' architecture for the rich and the cottage
style . . . no longer is the size of a house a symbol

Crow-Crocker, roof elevations

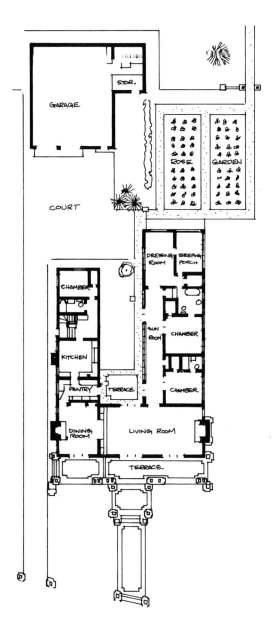

of its owner's position in the community . . . no longer . . . [is it] possible to judge the richness of a person's life and experience by the size of his house . . . no matter what their size or cost or for whom they were intended, [they] were beautiful to look at and easy to operate . . . they showed the same regard for the person who had to do the work. . . . The result was that by the time people were psychologically ready to accept the small house, it was already designed."

Jean Murray Bangs, "America Has Always Been a Great Place for the Prophet without Honor," *House Beautiful*, May 1950.

Crow-Crocker, plan

Crow-Crocker, chimney

76

7. BLACKER, MISS ANNIE, 675 South Madison Avenue 1912

Sometimes referred to as "the little Blacker House" to distinguish it from the impressive mansion done for a relative at 1177 Hillcrest. Original plans for this home were given to the Greene and Greene Library.

"Lovers of the latest in modern architecture are beating paths across Pasadena now to some dark and quiet houses that are 50 years old .... Today [these] ageless houses bring premium prices and are visited like shrines by young students of the 'new American style' in architecture."

Ray Duncan, "Pioneers in American Home Building," *The Pasadena Independent*, Scene, February 12, 1956.

"To explore all the forces which came to such a rewarding constellation in Greene and Greene's work is a job that must be left to some historian in love with the last golden years of the nineteenth century. It would be a rich and tangled pattern, big enough to include the William Morris and "manual arts" rebellion, burnt-wood pictures and Gilbert and Sullivan, as well as the first appearance of Japanese prints, the drift of the bungalow back from the British Colonies, the heady draught of suffragism which must have assisted the housewife in finally expressing her household needs, the great democratic passion that culminated in the Wilsonian freedoms. All this was part of the invigorating air of the period in which the roots of our native American architecture are to be found. In this period, the Greenes now take their proper place, somewhere near Sullivan and Wright."

Editor [Henry Wright, Managing Editor] *Introduction to*, Jean Murray Bangs, "Greene and Greene," *The Architectural Forum*, October 1948, p. 81.

Annie Blacker, entrance

8. SMITH, E. W., 272 South Los Robles Avenue
1910

This moderate sized two-story bungalow has been adapted for use by a financial firm, demonstrating an enlightened use of Pasadena's architectural heritage.

Herkimer Arms, trellis

E. W. Smith, front window and steps

9. BLACK, 210 South Madison Avenue   1903
Originally a very simple one-story cottage built for a teacher, it cost less than $3,000 and boasted some art glass. Extensive changes by Henry Greene in 1931.

10. HERKIMER ARMS, 527 Union Street
(See Earle, Mrs. J. Parker)   1913
Union was formerly Herkimer Street, and this 15-room apartment house, the only one known to have been designed by the Greenes, gives a clue to the degree of urbanization in Pasadena by 1913. Features are some built-in furniture, sculptured moldings above the windows, green Chinese tile inserts in the facade (now painted), and flanking arbors. Cost: $15,000. Compare with Williams residence in Altadena (Greene Walk 4).

"The Herkimer Arms Apartment," *California Southland* 30 (Pasadena) June 1922, described in an advertisement as providing "Comfort without extravagance" and as being "close in without noise."

11. SANBORN, 65 North Catalina Avenue 1904
Originally at 999 E. Colorado Blvd., this residence was moved north into a former orange grove in the 1930s. The present east entrance originally faced onto Colorado Boulevard. Interior changes over the years have eliminated any coherence in plan; it is now a men's boarding house.

Sanborn, not to scale; apparent plan

Sanborn, tower form

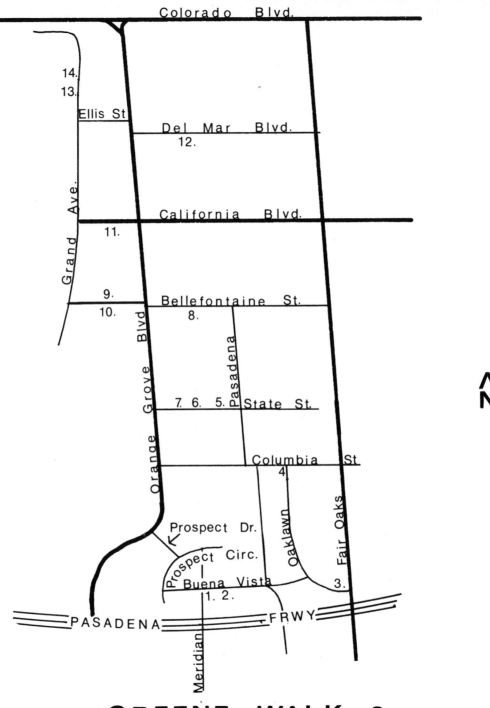

GREENE WALK 3

Longley, two windows

1. GARFIELD, 1001 Buena Vista Avenue, South Pasadena   1904
"The plot is level in the foreground, but declines so abruptly that the house was obliged to set its heels firmly to the ground below and then rise gracefully and show a pleasant face in front." ("A Chalet in Pasadena," *House Beautiful*, February 1906). Built for the widow of President James A. Garfield, this residence has the sloping, sheltering roof and oiled cedar shingles so typical of Greene and Greene structures at the crest of their career. A south sunroom overlooked the orange groves below, now eliminated by the Pasadena Freeway. On the National Register of Historic Places

2. LONGLEY, 1005 Buena Vista Avenue, South Pasadena   1897
The seven years' difference between this early eclectic frame house and its neighbor to the west reveal clearly the period of emerging Greene and Greene characteristics. Classical touches in pillars and windows indicate the East Coast Beaux Arts architectural school training, reflecting the experience of the architects before coming to Pasadena. This is

"Whereas the entrance to a Swiss chalet, for an American, is often difficult to discover, that of the Californian is given the place of honor directly at the front." Note posts on recessed boulders (suggesting the Oriental) flanking the entrance.

Dana, THE SWISS CHALET BOOK, p. 128.

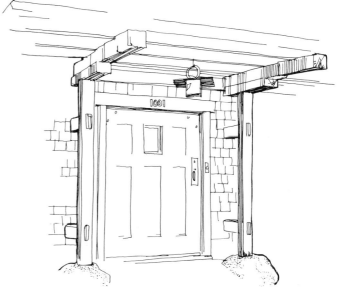

Garfield, entrance

81

believed to be the earliest Greene and Greene still standing. On the National Register of Historic Places.

3. BRIDGE, WAITING HOUSE, Oaklawn at Fair Oaks, South Pasadena   1906
There appears to be no evidence to support Greene and Greene identification for any of the residences on Oaklawn. The delightful roofed pedestrian gates at Columbia Street, the Waiting House at the Fair Oaks end of the bridge, and the walls along Columbia and Fremont set the tone for this residential development. The reinforced concrete bridge, 340 feet long, was originally designed without the center support, but skeptical officials retained a consulting engineer, and a change

was made, dismaying to the architects. Perhaps this is why they apparently did no further building in this tract. These three structures (see GATES, below) are registered South Pasadena Historical Landmarks, and the bridge and waiting station have been entered on the National Register of Historic Places.

See Saph, A. V., "A Discussion of a Reinforced Concrete Arch," *Architect and Engineer* 4 (San Francisco) August 1906. pp. 51-55. Commentary by an engineer on the reinforced concrete bridge with five arches of variable span and rise. Provides illustrations, plans, and a technical description of the construction of the Oaklawn Bridge.

Bridge, from park at Fair Oaks Avenue

Roofed gates at Oaklawn and Columbia Street,
lantern missing

4. GATES, Oaklawn at Columbia Street, South
   Pasadena   1906
   These roofed gates tie into the wall sections
   along Fremont and Columbia, some of which
   have been altered, and create an enclave that
   was well advertised during the period of their
   construction.

5. ROWLAND, 225 West State Street,
   Pasadena   1902
   Moved from 45 South Marengo in 1912, this
   eleven-room residence cost $6,000 and was
   designed with a separate entry and office for
   its physician client. Note recessed dormer
   window on the second floor. Originally un-
   painted; remodeling has enlarged the living
   room window. Dr. Rowland was a co-founder
   of the Pasadena Rose Parade.

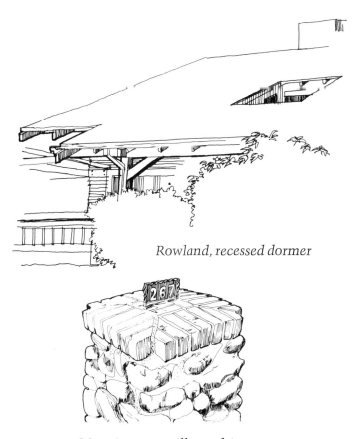

Rowland, recessed dormer

Merwin, stone pillar at drive

6. MERWIN, 267 West State Street,
   Pasadena   1904
   The classical pillars flanking the entrance
   were a request of the client, an Episcopal
   minister. Ecclesiastical designs on the front
   door and interior stair, and a study with its
   own entrance on the southwest corner per-
   sonalize this residence. The Reverend Merwin was a founder of the Twilight Club and
   assisted in establishing the South Pasadena
   Library. Appropriate new arbor.

7. PITCAIRN, 289 West State Street, Pasadena
1906

This house has a special strength and individuality, and a modest version of the second-floor porch which, on The Gamble House, seems to fling itself into space. Carefully positioned above grade, it was, until recently, graced by a wisteria vine of architectural proportions. The offset plan places dining room and a generous stair to the west, and a large two-story service block to the rear and farther west. Three slender windows at different levels mark the location of the service stair.

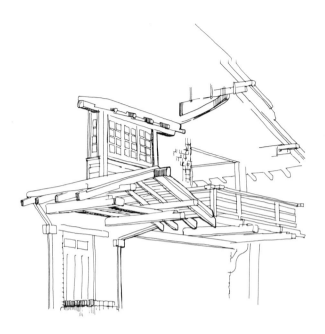

Pitcairn, facade

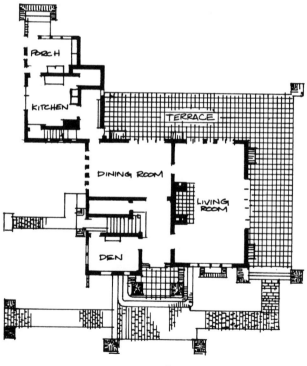

Pitcairn, plan

The cedar shingles and malthoid roof are familiar Greene and Greene features. Cost $14,000. Now adapted to use as an Art Center by Westridge School, its present owner.

"... The Picturesque point of view was predominantly visual rather than practical in its usual concerns. Asymmetrical massing allowed, even forced, asymmetrical planning, however, thereby encouraging functional differentiation of the disposition and the sizes of various rooms ...."

Henry-Russell Hitchcock, ARCHITECTURE: 19th & 20th CENTURIES, p. 255.

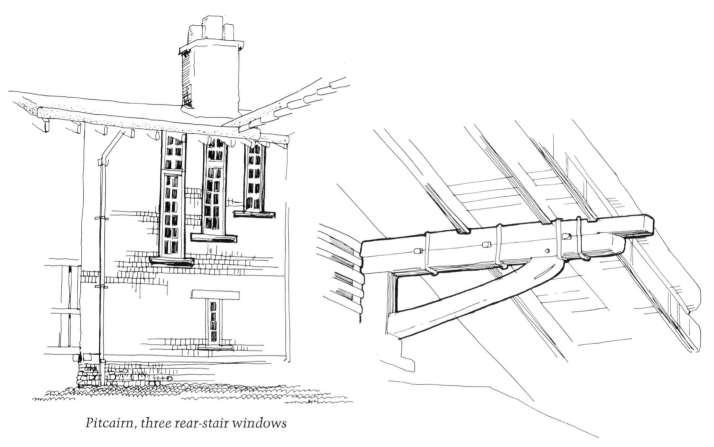

Pitcairn, three rear-stair windows

Pitcairn, knee brace

"... What lifted the architects above any movement was more than their sincerity, it was their understanding of a house as a total thing. In their work nothing stands out as detail although some of their solutions are miraculous. It is the inevitability of the solution which is astonishing. The purpose is always immediately evident...."

Esther McCoy, "Notes on Greene and Greene, *Arts and Architecture*, 70, July 1953, p. 38.

"... Conjuring with the Texture of Timber."

Wayne Andrews, ARCHITECTURE, AMBITION, AND AMERICANS, 1955, p. 274.

8. HOLLISTER, 310 Bellefontaine Street, Pasadena 1899
Another commodious frame house of the Greenes' early eclectic period. Upper porch was enclosed at a later date. Many small graceful touches inside and out.

9. PHILLIPS, 459 Bellefontaine Street, Pasadena 1906
Partially enclosed entrance pergola offers welcome scale to this large family home, comparable in size to the Arthur Libby residence on Orange Grove Blvd. just north of Bellefontaine, demolished in 1969. Present owners have done some careful remodeling.

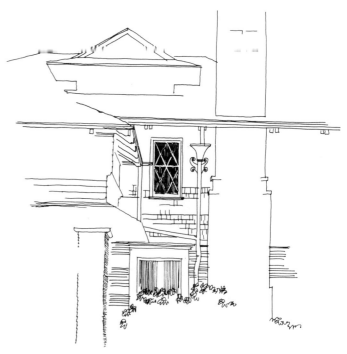

Hollister, drain pipe, diamond-pane window

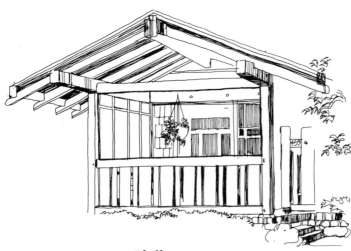

Phillips, entrance

"The Swiss Chalet today is to be found scattered here and there all over the globe. Its motive is of such elemental significance and character as to make its worth and desirableness recognized in any zone. The fundamental truth and unchanging beauty expressed by the broad protecting brim shading the almost human face of the wall below, are irresistible in their appeal. The Chalet motive is not Swiss; it is not Tyrolean, nor Himalayan. It is universal. And by reason of its inherent beauty it is adaptable to any site and any condition where land is plentiful, and where picturesqueness and harmony with the natural surroundings are the first considerations . . . ."

William S. B. Dana, THE SWISS CHALET BOOK, p. 127. 1913.

Ware, facade

10. WARE, 460 Bellefontaine Street, Pasadena
    1913

Designed for a client who desired a residence of English derivation similar to his home in the midwest. This eleven-room house has a living room oriented to a rear hillside garden and has an east front kitchen, unusual for this period. Early example of soffit lighting in the living room.

11. DE FOREST, 530 West California Boulevard, Pasadena
    1906

An excellent example of careful siting on a lot that drops steeply at the rear and allows an uninterrupted view from the living room across the treetops. An inglenook and two different porches, one open, one glazed, insure enjoyment of every kind of weather. The charming simplicity remains unchanged and the house is carefully maintained.

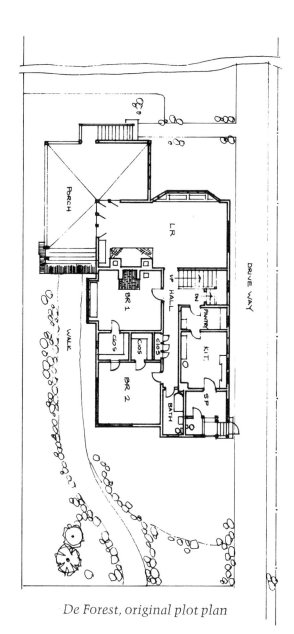

De Forest, original plot plan

De Forest, lantern, east window

"William Morris would have loved the house for its design and craftsmanship . . . here survives the lofty spirit of that paragon of American architectural magazines, *The Craftsman.*"

James Ackerman, *Architectural Record*, p. 203, February 1957.

88

12. BOLTON, 370 (Elevado) Del Mar Boulevard, Pasadena   1907

The second house built for Dr. Bolton, costing about $11,000, underwent "French Provincialization" in 1952, but retains many interesting features. Art glass in the front door has been removed for safekeeping by Ambassador College, its present owner, which uses the house for furniture storage. It has been unoccupied for some time. The rounded two-story bay window on the front is a later addition by Henry Greene for the Culbertson sisters, who moved to this smaller residence from 1188 Hillcrest in 1917.

". . . The spare, tight quality of the bay window is Henry Greene."

Robert J. Clark, correspondence, 1973
Bay window alteration, 1918

Bolton, tower bay window, entrance, window

13. FORD, 215 South Grand Avenue, Pasadena
1908

Although several sets of plans for Freeman Ford exist and include features later used in The Gamble House (a third floor, a pergola gate), a completion date of 1908 seems realistic for this $30,000 "bungalow." Originally the area at the entrance, the study, was approximately a story and a half; it was later lowered at the same time that the first roof (a kind of composition called malthoid) was replaced by tile. The open plan, surrounding a square tiled court with pool, is the Greenes' most sophisticated U-shaped plan. This exceptional residence overlooking the arroyo was called Linda Vista Rancho by the owner. Original tan color restored by owner. Curving drive and landscaped berms provide privacy from the street. Front entrance is not visible except to invited guests. See sketch.

Ford, front door

89

"The work which gave shape and grace to the widely built California Bungalow, which showed Americans how to employ their favorite building material, wood, with great honesty and vitality, had been completely overlooked by the professional schools and the architectural history books...."

Editor, in Introduction to Jean Murray Bangs, "Greene and Greene," *The Architectural Forum*, October 1948, p. 81.

"Over and over again I would reiterate that Modern is a point of view — not a style." William Wurster (p. 55, credit below).

"When I traveled across the country and through the East in 1935, I carried in my mind the impression made by an exhibit of Californian domestic architecture which I had seen just before I left [Honor Awards, San Francisco, 1934], and felt more and more strongly that the Californian product was as a whole fresher, franker and less style-bound than the work in any other part of the country...," mentioning that this was equally true of earlier years when he had seen the Greenes' work he continues with "But . . . it seems to me that the significant thing is not the influence of 'Modernism' on California architecture, but the influence of California on 'Modernism' . . . something more suave and gracious and peculiar to this more smiling land."

Howard Moise, Professor, School of Architecture, University of California at Berkeley, "Architect's Convention Retrospect," *Architect and Engineer*, 91, November 1936, pp. 52, 53.

[Professor Moïse's statement stands almost alone at a period when there was a dearth of comments of any kind!]

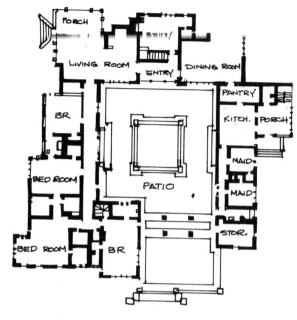

Ford, plan

"In Southern California the Spanish influence was plain in the house built around a patio which was the link between earth and walls. Here in an unroofed living room was combined privacy and outdoor living. This plan persists today because it is as valid as it was two hundred years ago...."

Esther McCoy, "West Coast Architecture: A Romantic Movement Ends," *Pacific Spectator*, p. 20 *ff*.

14. ROBINSON, 195 South Grand Avenue 1906
A shallow C in plan, stucco with wood trim
in material, this two-story residence is oriented to the rear arroyo view. At the south end
of the house is a charming garden room, once
an open porch with floral forms in tile. In
1917 the den was extended to become a library bringing the total cost to about $25,000.
A comparison between the dining room set
designed for this house (now in the Greene
and Greene Library) with that for The Gamble House, reveals clearly the changing form
of Greene and Greene designs between 1906
and 1909.

Robinson, lantern on gate post

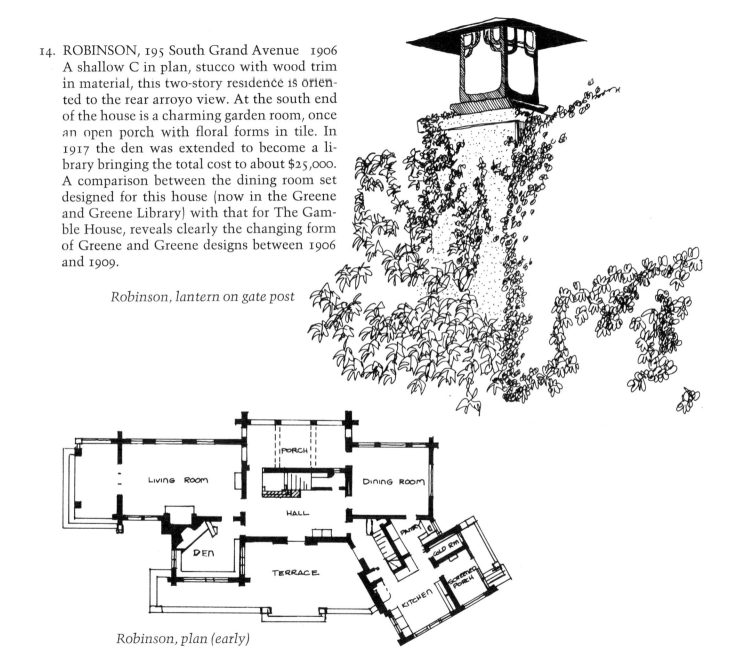

Robinson, plan (early)

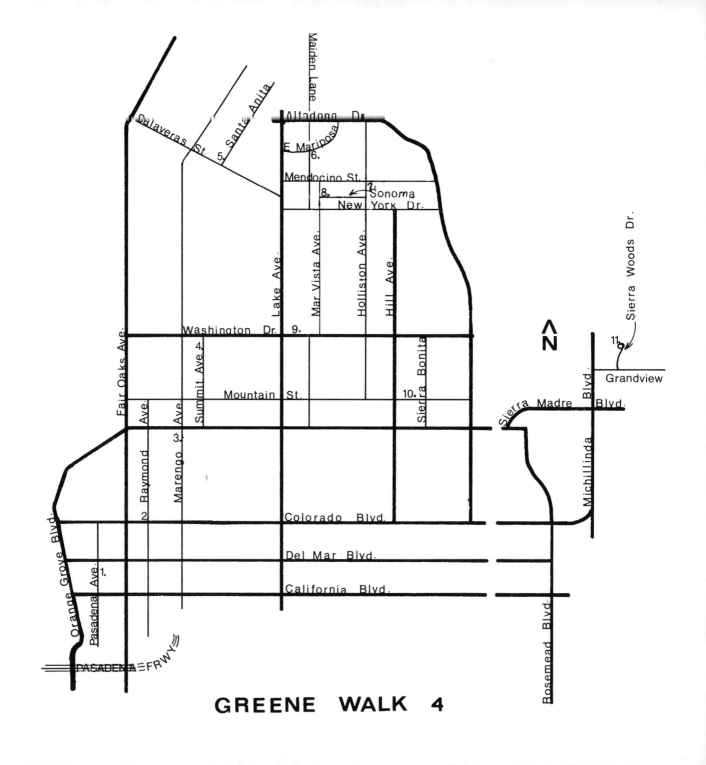

GREENE WALK 4

Greene Walk 4 — Around Town
(drive)

1. STALHUTH, 380 South Pasadena Avenue, Pasadena   1907
This small, inexpensive residence was designed for, and built by, the mason who worked for Greene and Greene on The Gamble House.

2. KINNEY-KENDALL, business block (63), 65 West Colorado Boulevard, Pasadena   1897
In 1896 the northwest corner of Raymond and Colorado was one of the most desirable business locations in Pasadena. Joseph N. Kinney of Maine, "through the enterprising agency of B. O. Kendall," engaged the Greenes to design a two-story block. The Pasadena Star of June 11, 1896, reports a change to a three-story building with a doubled Colorado Street frontage, "most satisfactory to the artistic eye and to the admirer of substantial and durable construction . . . [combining] two modern essentials, iron and glass, and in appearance light and graceful . . . ." The interior was to be painted Oregon pine and there would be no inside rooms. The first floor, stores and offices; the second floor, offices only; the third floor, to be occupied by the Odd Fellows. "The designs, it will be admitted, are very creditable to the taste and skill of our rising young architects, Messrs. Greene and Greene."

Kinney-Kendall, original structure

93

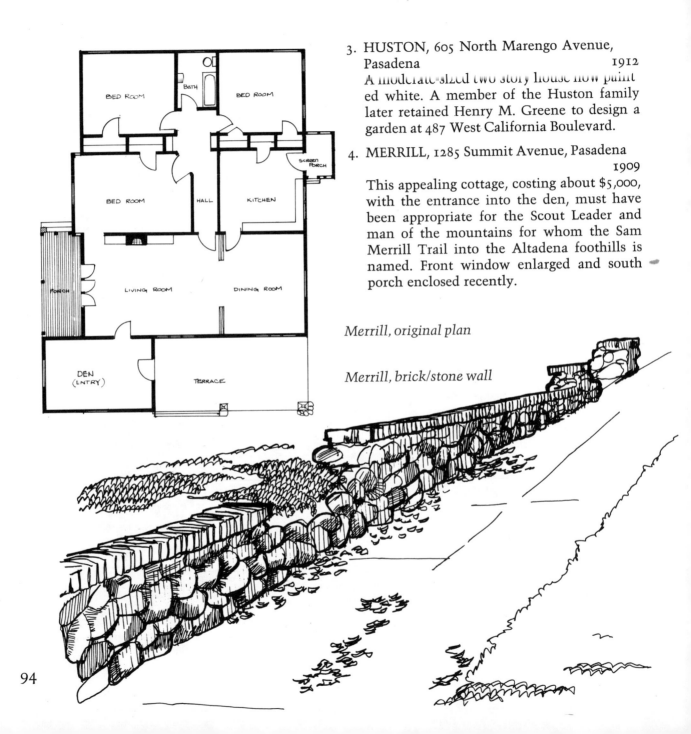

3. HUSTON, 605 North Marengo Avenue, Pasadena 1912
A moderate-sized two story house now paint ed white. A member of the Huston family later retained Henry M. Greene to design a garden at 487 West California Boulevard.

4. MERRILL, 1285 Summit Avenue, Pasadena 1909

This appealing cottage, costing about $5,000, with the entrance into the den, must have been appropriate for the Scout Leader and man of the mountains for whom the Sam Merrill Trail into the Altadena foothills is named. Front window enlarged and south porch enclosed recently.

Merrill, original plan

Merrill, brick/stone wall

BED ROOM

BATH

BED ROOM

SCREEN PORCH

BED ROOM

HALL

KITCHEN

PORCH

LIVING ROOM

DINING ROOM

DEN (ENTRY)

TERRACE

Bowen, angled bay window

5. BOWEN, 2425 North Santa Anita Avenue, Altadena   1905
The original entrance was at 443 East Calaveras Street. The extensive grounds around the outbuildings of this comfortable home were more productive at an earlier time when Altadena was rural ranch land. Originally it was a one-story house of seven rooms; it has undergone some interior remodeling and is now painted white.

6. BRANDT-SERRURIER, 1086 East Mariposa Street, Altadena   1906
This house, listed on plan as "Bungalow for A. C. Brandt at Pasadena," can be considered a speculation house for it was designed for a recognized contractor. It was formerly on the northeast corner. Mr. Serrurier, an inventor from Holland for whom the Greenes did at

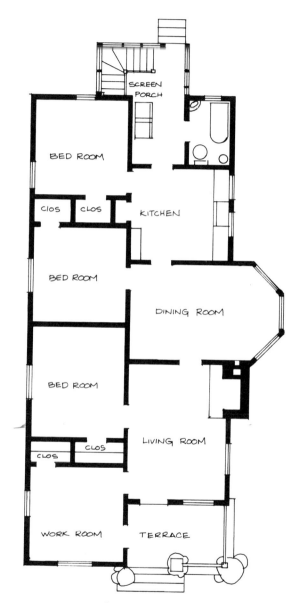

Brandt-Serrurier, early plan

Brandt-Serrurier, original design

least one other design, subdivided the Ganesha Tract. He lived in this house for a time, and later moved it across the street, when it became a rental. The living room has been extended, a garage added, and interior changes made.

7. SWAN, 2162 North Holliston Avenue, Altadena   1898
This amazingly large and elaborate commission for two young architects indicates the respect accorded them in Pasadena only four years after opening an office. It also reflects their training in the east and familiarity with the shingle style. "Torrington Place," moved from its prominent location at 515 East Colorado Boulevard (at Oakland) in 1925, is now plastered and somewhat altered, and the long roof slope on the right, which originally extended over the drive, has been cut close to the south side wall. It serves as a rest home and much of its gracious classical interior and exterior detailing is preserved. A sketch of this house as it appeared originally may be seen beside that of an earlier, eastern ancestor, the Low House.

". . . The Greenes began developing their design vocabulary while working within the limits of the conventional house. It grew in time into a language, which they were to use with great flexibility. . . ."

Esther McCoy, "Notes on Greene and Greene," *Arts and Architecture*, July 1953.

(a) Swan House, original natural shingles, 1898.
(b) Low House, by McKim, Mead and White, 1887, Bristol, R. I.

8. WILLIAMS, 1145 Sonoma Drive, Altadena
1916

Although the plans for this house carry the firm name of Greene and Greene, it was designed after Charles S. Greene had moved to Carmel. The stucco walls have the smooth-molded features first observed in the Herkimer Arms; it is different in form and materials from the usual Greene and Greene.

Williams, vent detail

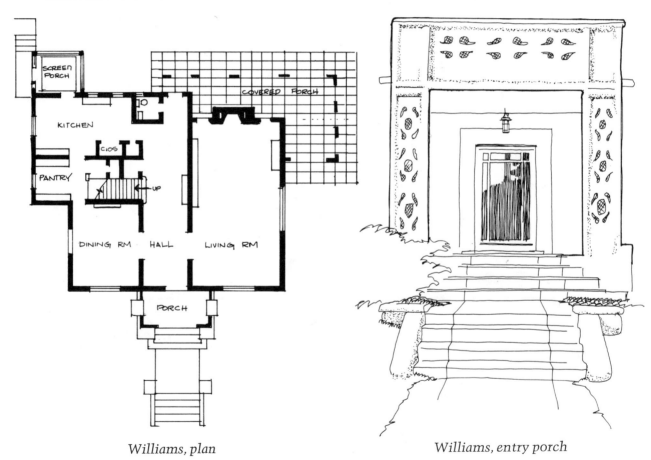

Williams, plan

Williams, entry porch

Longfellow School, original block

of the Municipal Water System." This residence, though not Spanish Colonial like many built in the twenties, has the tile roof and smooth stucco walls so popular after the eclipse of the shingle bungalow. There is a concrete soundproof vault that safeguarded a rare book collection. While Mayor Thum was in office, Henry Greene, with Grey and Roehrig and the city attorney, drew up a building code for Pasadena (Ordinance; 1913).

9. LONGFELLOW ELEMENTARY SCHOOL, 1065 East Washington Avenue, Pasadena
1912

Whether because of the specifics of the assignment or because they were unaware of the challenge of climate being met by other architects in school building (Hunt and Grey in Polytechnic School, Pasadena, 1903), this building, the Greenes' only school, lacks significance in either its rectangular form or plan. The nine-room, concrete, two-story fireproof building was considered "the most substantial addition" of that year in the *Annual Report* of the Pasadena City Schools. Cost: $38,000.

10. THUM, 1507 East Mountain Avenue, Pasadena
1925

Designed by Henry Greene for a former mayor of Pasadena (1911-1913) whose accomplishments earned him the title of "Father

Thum, entry

11. CAMP, 327 Sierra Woods Drive, Sierra Madre
1904

Designed for an attorney for the Santa Fe Railroad, who was also a member of the first City Council of Sierra Madre, this residence formerly relaxed at the top of the rise above Grandview, which was then devoid of other houses. Its address was formerly 497 Grandview. Descriptions and photographs of this house reveal it as the epitome of "A Mountain Bungalow." Later additions included a second story to the bedroom wing, reached by a generous central stairway and hall. Originally it was brown shingle. Its robust living room fireplace is one of the most appealing arrangements of natural materials (brick, wood, boulders) ever designed by the Greenes. "In the Camp House at Sierra Madre, Mr. Greene has given us one of the best adaptations of the feeling of the Swiss mountain house that we have in California. Whether it was intentional or not, Mr. Greene has sloped his roofs so that they almost exactly correspond to the slopes of the mountains in the background. This gives the house an unusual effect of fitness and makes it seem as though it belonged to the rest of the landscape." (Arthur Kelly, "California Bungalows," *Country Life in America*, May 1914.)

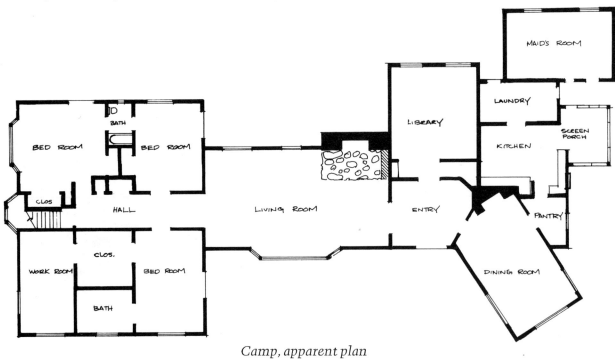

Camp, apparent plan

Camp, fireplace

"When American architecture sought regeneration it turned to Europe and elsewhere rather than to its own native soil. The indigenous quality of the Prairie School [and California Bungalow?] held little appeal during the interval between the wars. Only after 1945 was it rediscovered, when public taste again favored a low, small-scale, anti-monumental architecture, an architecture rooted in the earth. By then, however, continuity was broken, principles were forgotten, and the architects dead or dispersed. The features of the prairie house [and California Bungalow?], often ill-understood and debased, were incorporated into the promoter-built split-level or ranch-style houses of mid-century. Only in California, and more recently, in the Midwest, has the work of the early century inspired a younger generation in the direction of a new, vital course for American architecture."

H. Allen Brooks, THE PRAIRIE SCHOOL: FRANK LLOYD WRIGHT AND HIS MIDWEST CONTEMPORARIES, 1972, p. 348.

VI. Reading List

Starting in 1897, illustrations of Greene and Greene buildings appear in promotional literature for the Tournament of Roses. Most of these special publications, produced locally, are available at the Pasadena Historical Society, the Greene and Greene Library, and the Pasadena Public Library. These and other printed and illustrative sources are worth investigating for early views of Greene and Greene houses. However, there is often little text and Greene and Greene credits are irregular and occasionally in error. Beginning in 1902, popular and professional national magazines included their work with increasing frequency; this recognition wanes with the first war years. F. Morgan Yost's visit to the West Coast after World War II sparked a revival of interest that fanned the attention of numerous architects and architectural historians, resulting in a reappreciation of Greene and Greene. A chronological, comprehensive bibliography could provide fascinating details documenting not only Greene and Greene but the shifts in attitudes toward architecture from the turn of the century to the present time.

The relatively few entries selected for this Reading List are of considerable substance, usually illustrated and readily available. Also included is more general material that may serve to anchor the Greenes to the aesthetic and historical currents of the 19th and 20th centuries. Brief annotations should prove helpful; both the Greene and Greene Library and the Pasadena Public Library may provide additional resources.

Pages given are specific Greene and Greene references. Additional complete bibliographical information given in the footnotes to the Introduction is not repeated in the Reading List.

BOOKS

Andrews, Wayne, A SOCIAL HISTORY OF AMERICAN ARCHITECTURE: ARCHITECTURE, AMBITION AND AMERICANS, Chicago, The Free Press, new paperback ed., 1964, reprinted 1966. Pp. 274-276, 284, 287.
An authoritative, well-written presentation of many important American houses, including Pratt and Gamble.

Bailey, Stuart Wilder, "The Gamble House, 1908: An Analytical Description of a Residence in Pasadena, California, in View of Some of the Influences Affecting Its Design," M.A. Thesis, Claremont Graduate School, Claremont, Calif., Dec. 10, 1954. Bound in hard cover; in Greene and Greene Library. First comprehensive treatment of the Gamble House, with 33 pages of photographs by William R. Current.

Banham, Reyner, ARCHITECTURE OF THE WELL-TEMPERED ENVIRONMENT. London, Architectural Press, 1969, reprinted 1973. Pp. 102-104. References to Gamble House.

Banham, Reyner, LOS ANGELES: THE ARCHITECTURE OF FOUR ECOLOGIES. New York, Harper & Row, 1971. Pp. 58, 68-72. References to Blacker and Gamble houses. A provocative view of a city.

Brooks, H. Allen, THE PRAIRIE SCHOOL: FRANK LLOYD WRIGHT AND HIS MIDWEST CONTEMPORARIES. Toronto, Canada, University of Toronto Press, 1972. Pp. 21, 46, 344-345.
Thorough coverage of the Prairie School and parallel developments in other parts of the country.

Caldwell, John Wallace, "A Graphic and Historical Inquiry into the Furniture of Charles and Henry Greene," M.A. Thesis, Department of Fine Arts, Los Angeles State College of Applied Arts and Sciences, Los Angeles, Calif., January 1964. Bound in hard cover; in Greene and Greene Library. Two volumes.
An extensive treatment of Greene and Greene furniture with over 121 photographs. Furniture shown: Gamble, Pratt, Blacker, Bolton, Herkimer Arms Apartments, Ford, C. S. Greene, several unidentified pieces. Gamble House exterior, plan; exterior view of Pratt house.

Clark, Robert Judson, ed., The Arts and Crafts Movement in America 1876-1916. Handsome 10" x 13" catalog of 191 pages issued in connection with an exhibition organized by the Art Museum, Princeton University, and The Art Institute of Chicago. Princeton University Press, Princeton, New Jersey, 1972. Pp. 82-87.
References to Gamble, Blacker, Pratt and Thorsen houses; illustrations of Gamble house furniture and accessories.

Current, William R. and Karen, GREENE AND GREENE: ARCHITECTS IN THE RESIDENTIAL STYLE. Amon Carter Museum, Fort Worth, Texas, 1974. 128 pages. The first book on Greene and Greene. An essay, including 166 photographs of houses, plans, and furniture to accompany the traveling show opened at Amon Carter Museum, May 16, 1974. Morgan Press.

Embury, Aymar II, ONE HUNDRED COUNTRY HOUSES: MODERN AMERICAN EXAMPLES. New York, Century Co., 1909. Pp. 215-221. See Chapter XI, "Japanesque," for description and illustrations of Tichenor, Duncan-Irwin houses.

Fitch, James Marston, AMERICAN BUILDING: THE HISTORICAL FORCES THAT SHAPED IT. New York, Schocken Paperback ed., 1973. Pp. 232 234.

Gebhard, David; Montgomery, Roger; Winter, Robert; Woodbridge, Sally and John, A GUIDE TO ARCHITECTURE IN SAN FRANCISCO AND NORTHERN CALIFORNIA. Santa Barbara and Salt Lake City, Utah, Peregrine Smith, Inc., 1973. Pp. 264, 452, 460, 462.
Gives location of Greene and Greene houses in northern California. Authoritative Introduction.

Gebhard, David and Winter, Robert, A GUIDE TO ARCHITECTURE IN SOUTHERN CALIFORNIA. Los Angeles, California, Los Angeles County Museum of Art, 1965. Pp. 13, 85, 108-111, 120, 124-125, 151; Plates 14, 16, 18.
Gives location of 21 Greene and Greene houses. Revised edition to be published by Peregrine-Smith, Salt Lake City, Utah, October 1974.

Gebhard, David and Von Breton, Harriette, ARCHITECTURE IN CALIFORNIA 1868-1968. Santa Barbara, California, Standard Printing, 1968. Catalog. Pp. 4, 14, 55, 63.
Compact history, basic bibliography, chronological arrangement of illustrations of California buildings. References to Swan and Gamble houses.

Gowans, Allan, IMAGES OF AMERICAN LIVING: FOUR CENTURIES OF ARCHITECTURE AND FURNITURE AS A CULTURAL EXPRESSION. Philadelphia, Lippincott, 1964. Pp. 365, 389, 390, 393, 399, 402, 411, 412, 415, 429.
A cultural history including references to James Culbertson and Gamble houses.

Kirker, Harold C., CALIFORNIA'S ARCHITECTURAL FRONTIER: STYLE AND TRADITION IN THE NINETEENTH CENTURY. Santa Barbara and Salt Lake City, Utah, Peregrine Smith, Inc., 1973. Pp. xi-xiii, 128-129.
References to Greene and Greene and the California Bungalow.

Kornwolf, James D., M. H. BAILLIE SCOTT AND THE ARTS AND CRAFTS MOVEMENT. Baltimore, Johns Hopkins Press, 1972. Pp. 160, 345-346, 358, 360-361, 382.
Thorough text covering English origins of the Arts and Crafts Movement. Illustrations of Gamble house (interior, exterior, plan).

Lancaster, Clay, THE JAPANESE INFLUENCE IN AMERICA. New York, Walton H. Rawls, 1963. Pp. 106-117, 149, 152, 186, 224.
A beautiful book and a comprehensive treatment of the subject. Includes a discussion of the Bungalow and references to Bandini, Blacker, Cole, Duncan-Irwin, Gamble and Pratt houses.

McCoy, Esther, FIVE CALIFORNIA ARCHITECTS, Reinhold Publishing Corp., New York, 1960. Chapter on "Greene and Greene" by Randell L. Makinson. This popular book is available in almost every library and although out of print, will be reissued in paperback in the fall of 1974.

McWilliams, Carey, SOUTHERN CALIFORNIA: AN ISLAND ON THE LAND. Santa Barbara and Salt Lake City, Utah, Peregrine-Smith, Inc., 1973. Pp. 357-358. A new title, additional new preface; text reprinted from SOUTHERN CALIFORNIA COUNTRY, 1946.

Mumford, Lewis, ed., compilation, ROOTS OF CONTEMPORARY AMERICAN ARCHITECTURE. New York, Dover Publications, Inc., 1972. Pp. 12, 27.
An anthology of the American tradition providing excellent background; significant essays, biographical sketches.

Scully, Vincent J. Jr., THE SHINGLE STYLE AND THE STICK STYLE: ARCHITECTURAL THEORY AND DESIGN FROM DOWNING TO THE ORIGINS OF WRIGHT. New Haven, Yale University Press, revised edition, 1971. Pp. 157-158.
A delightful classic, by the authority on the history of shingle buildings.

Starr, Kevin, AMERICANS AND THE CALIFORNIA DREAM: 1850-1915. New York, Oxford University Press, 1973. Pp. 409-419, 412.
Excellent background material, although shy on architectural comments.

Whiffen, Marcus, AMERICAN ARCHITECTURE SINCE 1780: A GUIDE TO THE STYLES. Cambridge, Mass., MIT Press, 1969. Pp. 210, 212, 219, 221, 273.
Definitions and illustrations of various architectural styles, including Western Stick Style (Blacker house) and Bungaloid (Crow-Crocker house). A fine tool for the building watcher.

JOURNALS

Ackerman, James, "D. B. Gamble House, Pasadena, California," in "One Hundred Years of Significant Building. 9: Houses Since 1907," Architectural Record 121 (New York) February 1957. Pp. 199-206.

Bangs, Jean Murray, "America Has Always Been a Great Place for the Prophet without Honor," House Beautiful 92 (New York) May 1950. Pp. 128-139.
Article given Honorable Mention for the Howard Myers Memorial Award for Architectural Writing. Reprinted in Journal of the AIA, July 1952, under title "Prophet without Honor."

Bangs, Jean Murray, "A Parting Salute to the Fathers of the California Style," House and Home 12 (New York) August 1957. Pp. 84-95.

Bangs, Jean Murray, "Greene and Greene; The American House Owes Simplicity and Clarity to Two Almost-Forgotten Brothers Who Showed Us How to Build with Wood," Architectural Forum 89 (New York) October 1948. Pp. 80-89.
Well-written article, generously illustrated, with introduction by Henry Wright, Editor, in which he refers to the wide and benign influence of the Amer-

ican house when it made its appearance at the turn of the century. References to Thorsen, Pratt, Duncan-Irwin, C. Culbertson, Blacker houses.

Grey, Elmer, "Architecture in Southern California," *Architectural Record* 17 (New York) January 1905. Pp. 1-17.
A well-known Pasadena architect, contemporary with the Greenes, writes about the development of a distinctive Southern California architecture. Illustration of the patio of the Bandini house.

Hopkins, Una Nixon, "A House of Fine Detail that Conforms to the Hillside on Which It Is Built," *The Craftsman* 12 (New York) June 1907. Pp. 329-335. An illustrated description of Van Rossem house (No. 3). The first of many illustrated articles published in *The Craftsman* about the Greenes' work.

Hopkins, Una Nixon, "The Development of Domestic Architecture on the Pacific Coast," *The Craftsman* (New York) January 1908. Pp. 450-457. Illustrated description of Robinson, Libby, Garfield houses.

Keith, Henrietta, "The Trail of Japanese Influence in our Modern Domestic Architecture," *The Craftsman* 12 (New York) July 1907. Pp. 446-451. Illustrated description of Duncan-Irwin, C. S. Greene, White Sisters houses.

Lancaster, Clay, "My Interviews with Greene and Greene," *Journal of the AIA* 28 (Washington, D.C.) July 1957. Pp. 202-206.
A delightful description of a visit with Charles Greene in which he reveals the architect as artist and philosopher, and tells of the Oriental furniture and photographs, the drawings and paintings that were in the Studio. He also reports of a brief visit with an "alert" Henry Greene.

Lancaster, Clay, "Some Sources of Greene and Greene," *Journal of the AIA* 34 (Washington, D.C.) August 1960. Pp. 39-46. Reference to Duncan-Irwin, Blacker, Pratt houses.

Lancaster, Clay, "The American Bungalow," *Art Bulletin* 40 (New York) September 1958. Pp. 239-253. Reference to Bandini, Duncan-Irwin, Pratt, C. Culbertson houses.

Makinson, Randell L., "Greene and Greene: The Gamble House," and "An Academic Paper: The Gamble House," *The Prairie School Review* V (Park Forest, Ill.) Fourth Quarter, 1968. Pp. 4-23, 24-26, 31.

McCoy, Esther, "Notes on Greene and Greene," *Arts and Architecture* 70 (Los Angeles) July 1953. Pp. 27, 38. References to J. Culbertson, Duncan-Irwin houses.

McCoy, Esther, "West Coast Architecture: A Romantic Movement Ends," *Pacific Spectator* VII (Palo Alto) Winter 1953. Pp. 20-30. Commentary on the lack of recognition of California architects' contribution to the development of modern domestic architecture.

Winter, Robert, "American Sheaves from 'C.R.A.,'" *Journal of the Society of Architectural Historians* 30 (Philadelphia) December 1971. Pp. 317-322.
C. R. Ashbee, spokesman for the English Arts and Crafts Movement, visits America. References to C. S. Greene and Frank Lloyd Wright.

Yost, Lloyd Morgan, "Greene and Greene of Pasadena," *Journal of the Society of Architectural Historians* 9 (Philadelphia) March 1950. Pp. 11-19.
This is the first published article by Mr. Yost entirely on the Greenes' work, following his reference in "American Houses from Victorian to Modern," *American Lumberman and Building Products Merchandiser*, published in Chicago in September 1948, in which he refers to them as innovators of architectural design. References to Blacker, J. Culbertson, Gamble, Thorsen houses.

"A Fine Old House Remodeled with Respect," *House and Home* 9 (New York) March 1956. Pp. 180-184.
James Culbertson house, remodeled by Smith and Williams, including before and after plans.

"A New Appreciation of Greene and Greene," *Architectural Record* 103 (New York) May 1948. Pp. 138-149.
The first article about the Greenes to appear in a national architectural journal in the 40s. References to Bandini, Blacker, Crow, C. Culbertson, Gamble, Duncan-Irwin, Pratt houses.

"A New Life for a Grand Old Ruin," *House Beautiful* 98 (New York) February 1956. Pp. 88-95, 190, 192.
Reference to Tichenor house.

"Cordelia Culbertson Residence," *Pacific Coast Architect* 9 (San Francisco) March 1914. Pp. 10-11; 10 plates, on unnumbered pages. A detailed description of construction, furnishings.

"Discovering Our Recent Past," *House Beautiful* 99 (New York) December 1957. Pp. 152-163, 185.
Reference to James house (Carmel Highlands); Gamble house furniture shown with line of Dunbar Furniture designed from Greene & Greene models.

"Domestic Architecture in the West — California's Contribution to a National Architecture: Its Significance as Shown in the Work of Greene & Greene, Architects," *The Craftsman* 22 (New York) August 1912. Pp. 532-547.
References to Pitcairn, Hawks, Ranney, Blacker, Duncan-Irwin, Bolton, Robinson houses.

"Recognizing Our Own Architectural Traditions," *House Beautiful* 99 (New York) January 1957. Pp. 54-59, 106.
Reference to Gamble house.

"Some Pasadena Homes Showing Harmony between Structure and Landscape," *The Craftsman* 16 (New York) May 1909. Pp. 216-221.
References to C. S. Greene, Hawks, Ranney, Willet, Van Rossem-Neill houses.

"The House Set upon a Hill: Its Picturesque Opportunities and Architectural Problems," *The Craftsman* 26 (New York) August 1914. Pp. 532-539.
Description of Thorsen house.

"The Undiscovered Beauty of Our Recent Past," *House Beautiful* 99 (New York) January 1957. Pp. 48-53.
Reference to James house.

NEWSPAPERS

Starting February 9, 1947, C. Fred Shoop's Sunday column, Auld Lang Syne, in the *Pasadena Star-News* dealt at considerable length with various aspects of Pasadena history. Frequently these columns, which ran until 1965 (with rare interruptions), were based on interviews with senior residents of Pasadena and their recall of old events, buildings or personalities. Those columns in which the Greenes figure prominently are listed:

February 3, 1952 — "Early Day Pasadena Architects Influence California Homes," p. 24, refers to L. Morgan Yost, Jean Murray Bangs, and Blacker house.

June 1, 1952 — "Pasadena Developers of California Type Homes To Be Honored," p. 26, refers to tour that day and address by Henry Eggers, Architect.

August 1, 1955 — "Greene and Greene: Ahead of Their Time," refers to Mr. and Mrs. Hill, and Blacker house.

October 16, 1955 — "Citrus Ranching Wasn't Easy in the Early Days," concerns Leffingwell Ranch in Whittier, showing ranch building designed by Greene & Greene.

April 22, 1956 — "Architecture Stands the Test of Time Here," refers to 50th anniversary of some Greene & Greene homes, showing photograph of Irwin house in a snowstorm.

September 22, 1957 — "Pasadena Mansions Object of Home Tour," refers to the AIA Centennial Home Tour to start October 26. James Culbertson and Blacker houses are pictured.

July 27, 1961 — "Bandini Home Recalls Past," refers to fire destroying all but west wing in 1918, rebuilding to original plans in frame and stucco in 1925.

August 1, 1962 — "Freeway to Take a Greene & Greene [Unconfirmed] Home," refers to old Canright house built in 1901.

Bangs, Jean Murray, "Los Angeles — Know Thyself," *Los Angeles Times* Home Magazine (Los Angeles, Calif.) October 14, 1951. Pp. 4-13, 16, 18, 20, 39, 40, cover drawing.
Another extensive treatment of the Greenes' work, generously supported with photographs. Gamble, Bandini, Ford, Pratt, Tichenor, Duncan-Irwin, Nathan Bentz houses.

McCoy, Esther, "In Architecture — Who Starts a Style?" *Los Angeles Times* Home Magazine (Los Angeles, Calif.) July 19, 1953.
James Culbertson ("The California House: 1897"), Duncan-Irwin ("The California House . . . How It Started").

"Historic Project on Way: Gamble House Plan Outlined," *Pasadena Star News* (Pasadena, Calif.) April 22, 1966. P. 17.
Preservation and use of The Gamble house. Contract dedicates the land, buildings, and furnishings to Pasadena. University of Southern California to use building for 99 years, agrees to maintain interiors for city. City and University to share use. Advisory Board to oversee operations. USC students on Gamble Fellowships to reside in House.

MISCELLANEOUS

San Francisco Museum of Art, *Domestic Architecture of the Bay Region*. San Francisco, Calif., 1949. Np.
Exhibition held in San Francisco Museum of Art, September 16-October 3, 1949. Catalog includes essays by Lewis Mumford, William Wurster, Elizabeth Thompson, Clarence Mayhew, Francis Joseph McCarthy, etc. Lewis Mumford in "The Architecture of the Bay Region," deals with the vigorous tradition of modern building that took root in California a half-century ago. He concludes the exhibition repaired a serious omission in the histories of American architecture.

McCoy, Esther, *Roots of California Contemporary Architecture*. Los Angeles, Calif., The Los Angeles Art Commission and The Municipal Art Department, 1956. Pp. 2-3, 5, 8-9.
Work of Gill, Greene & Greene, Maybeck, Neutra, Schindler, Wright; Exhibition in Barnsdall Park, Los Angeles, September 9 through September 30, 1956. Catalog contains material that stimulated publication of FIVE CALIFORNIA ARCHITECTS. Reference to Gamble, Pratt houses.

California Arts Commission, *Seven Decades of Design*. Long Beach Museum of Art, Long Beach, Calif., 1967. Np.
Catalog for an exhibition shown in Long Beach (July 31 through September 10, 1967) and other cities in California. A survey in seating design. References to Gamble house furniture.

Gamble House Press Book, 2 vols. — Compiled by Myrtle Clark, first Greene and Greene Library Chairman, consisting of materials pertinent to public history of The Gamble House.

Greene and Greene Notebooks, 2 vols. — Compiled by Josephine Pletscher, Librarian, Fine Arts Coordinator, Fine Arts Room, Pasadena Public Library, Pasadena, Calif. Assembled starting in 1966/1967, containing Bibliography, Structure List, newspaper and magazine articles, brochures, research paper, tours, etc.

Brown, Robert Gregory, "The California Bungalow in Los Angeles: A Study in Origins and Classification," M.A. Thesis, Department of Geography, University of California, Los Angeles, 1964. Pp. 26-29.
Text and illustrations of the many varieties of the bungalow form and the Greenes as originators of the bungalow design.

Strand, Janann, "Oriental Influences in the Gamble House," original drawings by Gretchen Bernhard, research report, 1970, for University of California, Los Angeles, Greene and Greene Library, Pasadena Public Library, Greene & Greene Notebooks.

Hancock, Janet, "The Cordelia Culbertson House," research report for 1973 *Showcase of Interior Design* for the Pasadena Junior Philharmonic Committee, Pasadena, Calif. Greene and Greene Library, The Gamble House, Pasadena, Calif. C. Culbertson-Prentiss residence was 1973 Showcase House.

Cultural Heritage Committee (City of Pasadena), *11 Walks for You to Take in Pasadena.* Historic Preservation Week, May 8, 1973.
Brief histories and line maps. Several Greene & Greene houses on tours: Bentz, Gamble, Robinson, C. S. Greene, Van Rossem-Neill, White Sisters, Prospect Park Portals, C. Culbertson, Blacker. Brochure available at Pasadena City Hall, Pasadena Chamber of Commerce, libraries, etc.

"Pioneers of Modern Architecture," *Environmental Communications* (Venice, Calif.) May 1973.
Sets of slides to be purchased; 20 on Greene and Greene, including Gamble, Blacker houses.

Gamble House Docent Council: Schools Committee, *Schools Program Loan Packet.* Materials are compatible with all grade levels on the development of modern architecture and its relation to Pasadena's architectural heritage. The packet contains instructional materials and visual aids (38 slides). Contact Greene and Greene Library.

Tichenor House, recessed wall section

VII. Greene and Green Library

THE GREENE AND GREENE LIBRARY, located in the aerie on the top floor of The Gamble House, contains much of the information in this book. Although the concept of a library at The Gamble House had been advanced by a Docent and Professional Librarian, Myrtle Clark, in 1967, the idea was given additional scope by the Curator, Randell Makinson. It was at first called the Greene and Greene Library and Museum but the word *Museum* was dropped because it was misleading. The Library was dedicated in 1968; its development is largely due to funds, efforts, and acquisitions of the Docent Council of The Gamble House, building upon initial gifts from the Greene and Gamble families. Since that time there have been many other benefactors.

Essential to a research library are source materials, the original, primary stuff about which the rest of the contents revolve. Specifically, the source materials in the Greene and Greene Library are architectural drawings, periodicals, letters, photographs, awards, documents, books, manuscripts, and Greene and Gamble memorabilia. While there is relatively little source material in the Greene and Greene Library, the Library exists within a setting of the most important source material, the structures themselves.

Although the Greenes had commissions from Vancouver to San Diego, the greatest concentration of structures is in Pasadena, California.

Roughly one-third of the Greene and Greene source material is housed in the Architectural Documents Collection, School of Environmental Design, at the University of California at Berkeley, California; given by the C. S. Greene family in Carmel, it is well catalogued and cared for. Another third, consisting mainly of original drawings and blueprints, is in the Avery Architectural Library at Columbia University, New York City, and represents effects of the firm of Greene and Greene that had been in the custody of Jean Murray Bangs. A few drawings are in the AIA Library, Washington, D. C. The remainder, in private ownership in this and other areas, is not readily available to the public.

One unique contribution of the Greene and Greene Library, however, may be the development of a cross-index to materials housed elsewhere. There are many missing bits of information, but at present, file cards reveal where the architectural drawings for a particular residence are located, the names of most of the clients for whom furniture was commissioned, and where early photographs of a residence can be found. This Greene and Greene Comprehensive File can become a clearing house for information about the Greenes. Records show that most of the people who have made use of the Greene and Greene Library have come in search of material on the Greenes and their work.

The Greene and Greene Library is also a repository for the ever-growing quantity of published material about the Greenes, a developing Art Nouveau collection, material bearing on the

Arts and Crafts Movement with special emphasis on the development of the bungalow, Tiffany art forms, Stickley furniture, and other crafts; and a developing slide collection. Fundamental to the entire collection are general works concerning architecture and Pasadena and its history.

Reeve House, front door

VIII. About the Gamble House

THE GAMBLE HOUSE is the one Greene and Greene in prime condition that is open to the public on a regular basis. The residence and its furnishings were given by the Gamble Family to the City of Pasadena in 1966, after three generations of use. It is administered by the University of Southern California in a unique joint agreement with the City.

The Gamble House is situated one-half mile north of Colorado Boulevard (Interstate Highway 134, Route 66) on Westmoreland Place, a private street parallel to Orange Grove Boulevard, between Arroyo Terrace and Rosemont. (Enter by short drives cut through the north side of the 300 block of Orange Grove Boulevard.)

Guided tours of The Gamble House are open to the public each Tuesday and Thursday between 10 a.m. and 3 p.m. except for major holidays. On one Sunday in the spring and one in the fall there is an Open House Tea and Tour. Tour fees are $1 per person. Children under twelve accompanied by an adult, students, and military personnel are admitted free of charge with identification. All tours are conducted by Docents of The Gamble House.

The Greene and Greene Library in The Gamble House is a small, specialized research library. It is open to the public by appointment only, staffed by the Docent Council, and arrangements may be made by calling 213-793-3334.

Resolution 795, September 8, 1970, designates The Gamble House as a Cultural Heritage Landmark in Pasadena. It is a State Historical Landmark, and is listed in the National Register for Historic Buildings.

Gamble House, rear elevation

IX. The Docent Council

IN APRIL OF 1966 Sam T. Hurst, Dean of the School of Architecture and Fine Arts of the University of Southern California, asked Janann Strand to form a Docent Council for The Gamble House. With co-founder Dorothy Byles, many possible arrangements were considered. Four prominent docent groups in the Los Angeles area provided information about their purpose, function, and training. Three crucial points, common to all four groups, emerged; these appeared to insure a continued high level of commitment, service, and development:

1—That prospective docents be sponsored by someone familiar with the aims and activities of the group; that they be fully informed of the training, duties, and amount of service expected; that each then send a letter of commitment to acknowledge this understanding.

2—That a thorough, sustained training course be conducted, with regular attendance expected.

3—That there be continued opportunity for research and additional projects to deepen and extend the docents' knowledge, and to insure the vitality of the group.

Conforming to the definition of docent*, the initial members of this group were assured their role was to be scholarly and developmental rather than social or fund-raising. Continued close association with the University and community was urged by the Dean. Tentative preparations along these lines paralleled other plans for the opening of The Gamble House to the Public, and there were opportunities to refresh some knowledge of Greene and Greene and visit various structures.

Since there was at first no pattern for the many activities of the House, nor for the six thousand visitors who made their way to No. 4 Westmoreland Place that year, the Charter Docents did whatever was needed: guided the visitors, answered the phone, arranged the flowers, reorganized the basement, cleaned the third floor, refinished the furniture, outlined the training course, took inventory, acknowledged the acquisitions, gave special tours and lectures, and received out-of-town guests. A Library, quality publications, a Friends of The Gamble House group, and educational programs for the schools and immediate community were among the early suggestions of the initial docents. The present roster numbers about ninety and a new class of sponsored applicants has been trained each year.

Beginning in January 1967 and meeting on consecutive Mondays, the first docent training course at The Gamble House drew well-known authors and lecturers from many campuses and covered art, history, and architecture. Dr. David Gebhard of the University of California at Santa Barbara, Dr. Robert Winter of Occidental College, Deans Arthur B. Gallion, Sam T. Hurst and Crombie Taylor of the University of Southern California, and Esther McCoy, architectural historian and author, spoke that first year. The lectures on Greene and Greene have been the special province of the Curator of The Gamble House.

*Docent: a teacher or lecturer at certain universities who is not a regular faculty member; a knowledgeable guide; from the Latin docere, to teach.

NOTE ABOUT THE AUTHOR

JANANN STRAND, who started her term as the first Docent president at the close of the first training class in June of 1967, has contributed appropriate furnishings, manuscripts, lectures, refinishing, and two research files for the Greene and Greene Library. An Area File, consisting of an identifying photo and salient information about each Greene and Greene structure, organized by geographical areas, was begun as an adjunct to Greene Walks; the Greene and Greene Comprehensive File, developed from personal knowledge of material at both Avery Architectural Library and, with Megs Meriwether, at Berkeley. By attending classes on several campuses, she has made concerted efforts to expand the architectural knowledge of the Docents along with her own, and to bridge the history of the period between 1909, the date of The Gamble House, and 1974. Special tours and Greene Walks have been her particular province and this book provides one way of sharing this delight with a greater number, especially the many Greene and Greene enthusiasts in Pasadena.

NOTES

Please fill this blank with data for an outline of your biography, and return by mail at your early convenience to Chas. F. Lummis, Librarian, Public Library, Los Angeles, California.

For the LOS ANGELES PUBLIC LIBRARY'S DEPARTMENT OF
"Western History-Material."

This data is not for a book, but to file for reference as part of local history. These archives are to include biographies and portraits of all prominent citizens, living and dead. Your photograph should be filed also.

☞ The Palace Studio, 351 So. Broadway, will make a portrait of you for these files, free of charge.

Name in full _Henry Mather Greene,_

Chief Occupation _Architect_

Date of beginning it _Began to practice January 1894_

Address _146 Bellefontaine, Pasadena, California_

Place of Birth _Cincinnati, Ohio_

Date of Birth _January 23d 1870_

Parents { Father _Thomas Sumner Greene,_
{ Mother (maiden name in full) _Lelia Ariana Mather G._

Dates of your Father's Birth (and death) _September 19th 1842_

Dates of your Mother's Birth (and death) _November 4th 1844_

Names of her Parents _Oscar F. Mather Augusta Giles Wright Mather_

Important Ancestors, Paternal or Maternal _Cotton Mather_

Married or unmarried

If Married, to whom (full name) _Emeline Augusta Dart_

Date of Marriage _August 22d 1899_ Place _Rock Island, Ill._

Education (when and where) in detail. Give name, place and dates of public and private schools, academies, colleges, business and technical schools attended, with degrees conferred (if any), and dates of graduations (if a graduate).

St. Louis Public Schools; St. Louis Manual Training School, Class 1888; Massachussetts Institute of Technology Two Year Course 1890-

(OVER)

Military, Political and Civic Record

When did you come to California or the Southwest—From where? _Came to California September 1893 from Boston, Massachussetts._

Learned and Technical Societies, Titles, Decorations, Etc. _Associate Member of the American Institute of Architects; Member Southwestern Society of the Archeological Institute of America – Member Southern California Chapter American Institute Architects._

Social, Political, and other important Clubs and Associations (member of) _Corona Lodge #324, Masonic; Twilight Club;_

Religious Denomination

Politics _Republican_

School of Practice (if a physician)